Production	Lee Anne Singh
Research	Triphine Miyanda
	Priscilla Yosa
	Robyn Burton
	Chama Mwansa
Photography	Penny Dale
	Marek Patzer
	National Archives
	Nick Aslen
	Karien Joosten
	Zambia Information Services
	Francois d'Elbee
Editor	Penny Dale
Text	Jifipa Ngalande
Maps	Peter Jones
Layout & design	Vandita Varjangbhay
Printed by	Ultra Litho, SA

MW01530783

In the course of our research for the Magic of Zambia, we have been blessed with the help of so many people, family, friends and colleagues who have given us unwavering support and encouragement. It is difficult for us to mention everyone but we would like to thank all of those who made our research such pleasure and fun.

We would particularly like to thank Satwant Singh, for his support. His abundant knowledge of the country has been a great stimulation in identifying the hidden treasures of Zambia.

Special thanks to Ashok Varjangbhay for tolerating the production team throughout the process. Others who deserve specific mention are Dr Fay Gadsden, Rosanna Price Nyendwa, Anthony Morrison, Linda Shenton, Karien Kermer Joosten, Nick Aslen and Lyn Shaw for their advice and guidance in bringing this guide book to fruition.

IMAGE
PROMOTIONS

"Produced with the financial assistance of the
European Development Fund, EDF,
with the support of the
Centre for the Development of Enterprise, CDE (EU/ACP)"

DELEGATION OF THE EUROPEAN COMMISSION in Zambia
Plot 4899, Los Angeles Boulevard, LUSAKA
Telephone: 00 260 1 251140
Telefax: 00 160 1 252336

P.O. Box 34871, Lusaka, Zambia
Email: Delegation-Zambia@cec.eu.int
Web: www.delzmb.cec.eu.int

CONTENTS

LIKUMBI LIYA MIZE CEREMONY

HARRISON PHIRI, VIMBUZA DANCE, TUMBUKA PEOPLE

CONSTRUCTING A FOOD STORAGE

London
Berlin
Kiev
Paris
Rome
Athens
Ankara
Madrid
Tehran
Casablanca
Algiers
Tunis
Tel Aviv
Tripoli
Cairo
Riyadh
Timbuktu
Dakar
Khartoum
Freetown
Lagos
Accra
Kampala
Nairobi
Kinshasa
Dar-es-Salaam

ZAMBIA

Lusaka
Windhoek
Harare
Antananarivo
Johannesburg
Maputo
Durban
Cape Town

*H*ills wrapped in dense, emerald woods humming with bird and insect songs, a sparkling expanse of sapphire lakes with golden beaches, abundant waterfalls fed by rushing rivers, vast national parks where the lions roam free across a sea of tawny grass, the haunting cry of the fish eagle as it dives down to scoop up a luckless rainbow fish, this is Zambia.

Endlessly absorbing and exciting, Zambia's raw edge will leave the independent traveller breathless while luxurious lodges hidden away in a remote hypnotic wilderness guarantee a holiday of a lifetime for the more well-heeled tourist.

Zambia is a land of the fantastic and unexpected and the more you explore this huge country the more you realise how much one of Africa's undiscovered gems has to offer.

Venture into the bush, and you find a landscape littered with reminders of the past: ancient rock paintings, burial sites and small villages of thatched-roof huts that have been in the same area since the Iron Age.

This is the Africa of old, where life has followed a similar pattern over the ages: women pounding maize for the evening meal with babies wrapped in multi-coloured chitenge cloth slung on their backs, small children herding cattle, men in dugout canoes fishing, and colourful ceremonies to mark the harvest, new moon or the passage into adulthood.

Of course, modern Zambia is creeping into even the remotest villages but it is in the cities where change is most evident.

Lusaka is trying, with some success, to transform

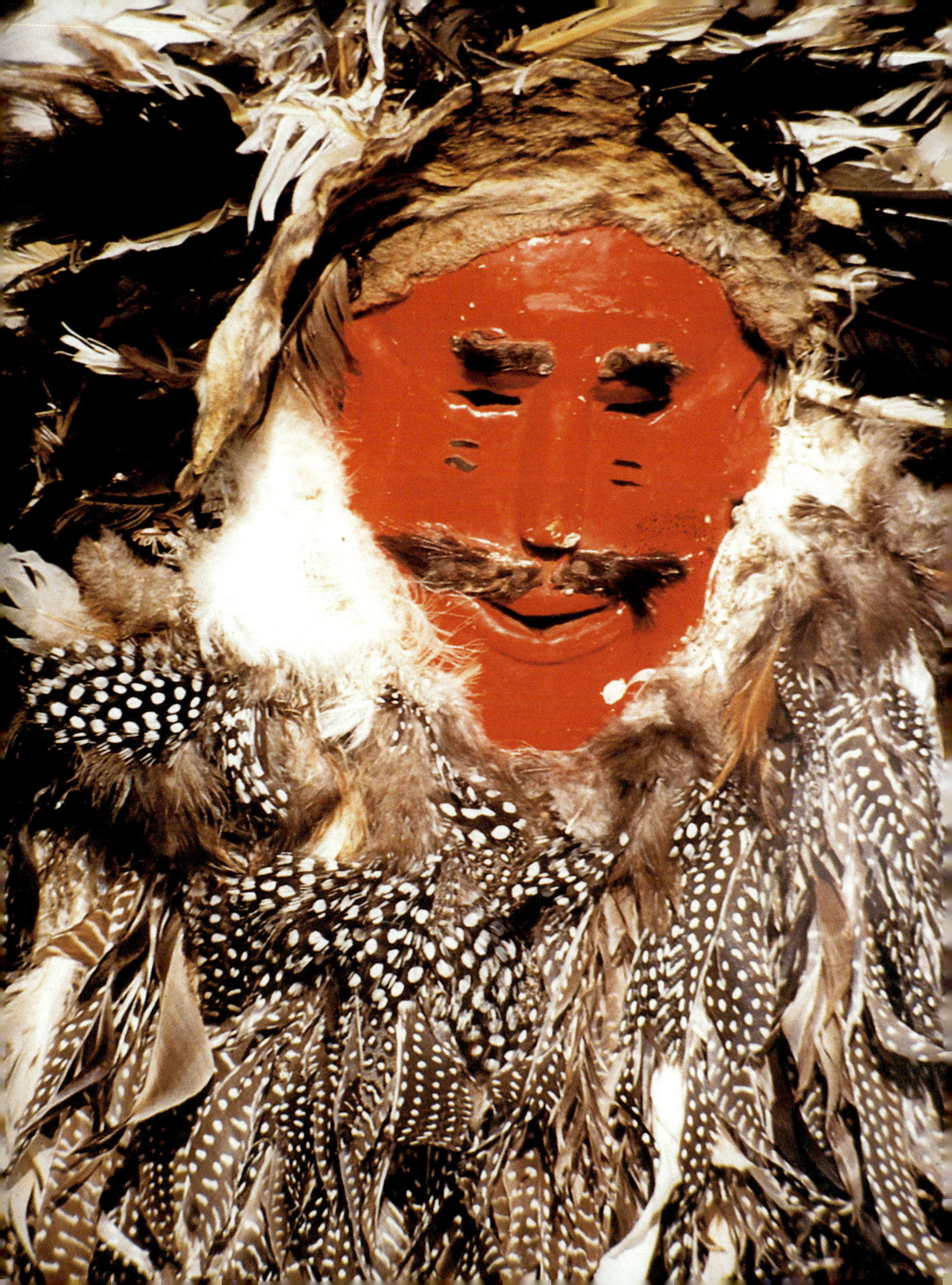

itself from a down-at-heel African capital into a glitzy metropolis. But it is the people who are the country's greatest treasure. With 73 different languages, Zambia is a rich cultural mosaic. Take a walk off the beaten track and you'll be rewarded with friendliness and curiosity.

Although most visitors are drawn to the country by its natural beauty, their enduring memory is likely to be of the Zambian people and their way of life.

Long after the memory of the country's wonderful sights have faded, even the most jaded traveller will remember the dignity, warmth and hospitality of Zambians.

LIKISHI DANCER - LIKUMBI LIYA MIZE CEREMONY

Provinces of Zambia

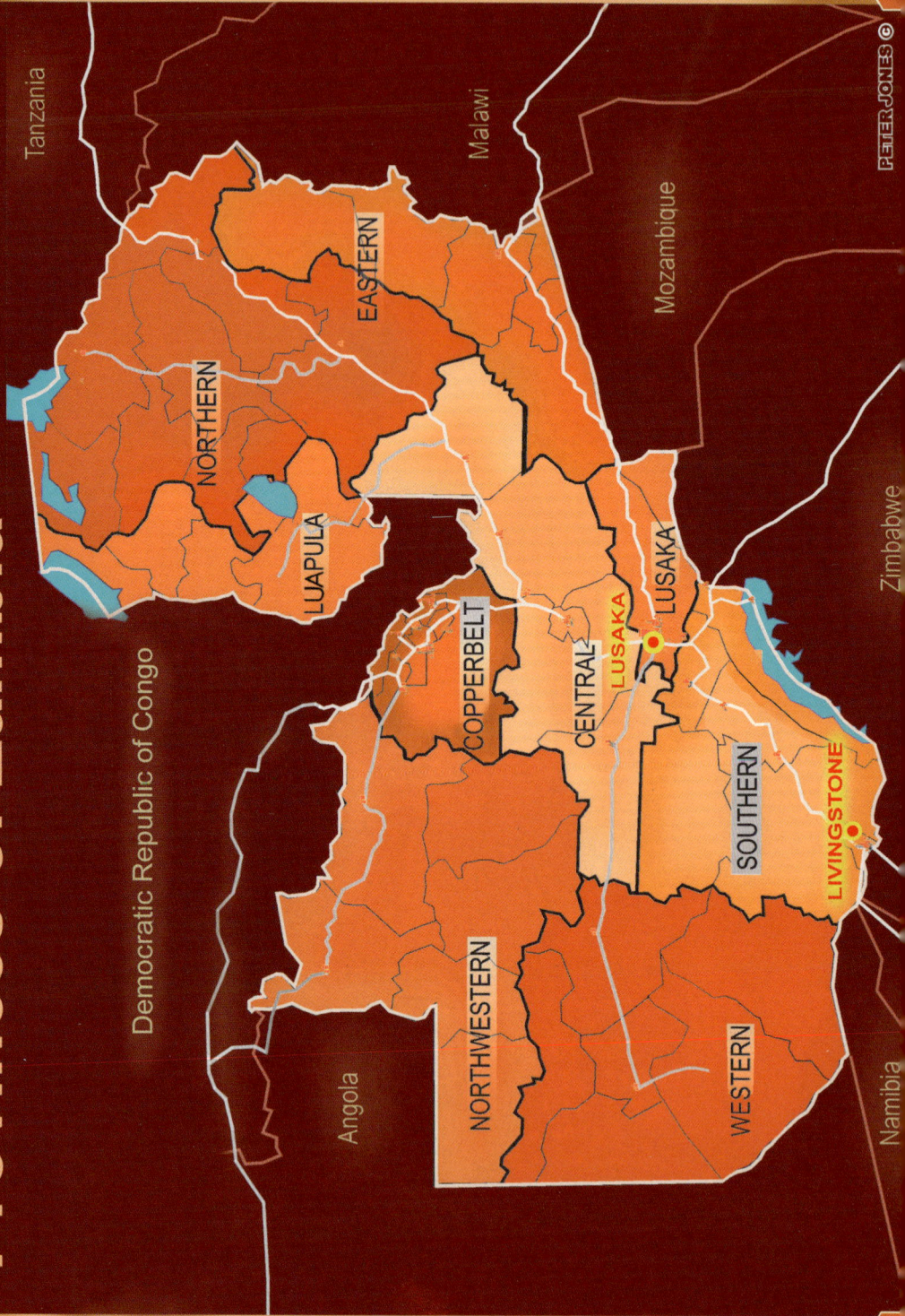

Tanzania

Malawi

Mozambique

EASTERN

NORTHERN

Democratic Republic of Congo

LUAPULA

COPPERBELT

CENTRAL

LUSAKA

LUSAKA

Zimbabwe

SOUTHERN

LIVINGSTONE

NORTHWESTERN

Angola

WESTERN

Namibia

PETER JONES ©

HISTORY

Zambia's human history stretches back millions of years, and is recorded in the country's many archeological sites.

The oldest Stone-Age sites in Zambia are near Livingstone, especially on the cliffs of the Batoka Gorge overlooking the Zambezi River.

Zambia's most fêted early inhabitant lived about 100,000 years ago and is known as Broken Hill Man, named after the mine near the town of Kabwe where he was discovered in 1921.

Between the twelfth and eighteenth centuries ancestors of today's Bantu-speaking tribes migrated to Zambia from the Luba-Lunda empire in Democratic Republic of Congo to form kingdoms alongside the older chiefdoms.

From their bases on the east coast of Africa, Swahili and Arab traders pushed into the interior, using the most obvious route of the Zambezi River, bartering salt and guns with the local Bantu people for gold, ivory and slaves. Some Swahili are thought to have settled at the confluence of the Luangwa and Zambezi Rivers in the south-east of modern Zambia.

The first Europeans, traders from Portugal, reached Zambia only in the late eighteenth century. Their arrival was one of a series of changes and upheavals that began to break the isolation of the vast untapped tract of land between the Zambezi River and Lake Tanganyika.

In the early nineteenth century, tribes fleeing the military might of Shaka and his Zulu fighting machine in present-day South Africa scattered across southern Africa. The Makololo people raided the Tonga of south-west Zambia and eventually briefly ruled over today's Lozi people while the Ngoni settled in eastern Zambia.

It was the tales of the Scottish explorer and missionary David Livingstone — who explored large parts of Zambia looking for navigable rivers on which the steam ships could carry cargo and missionaries to introduce Christianity, which really put this part of Africa on the world map and indirectly sparked the 'Scramble for Africa' by European powers.

The Berlin Conference of 1884-85 saw Africa formally carved up between France, Germany, Belgium, Portugal and Britain, which got the lion's share including present day Zambia.

COLONIAL TIMES

Eager to cut down on the running costs of the new colonies, in 1889 Britain agreed to an offer made by diamond magnate Cecil Rhodes and handed over Zambia's administration to his British South Africa Company (BSAC).

The new colony, named in honour of Rhodes, was initially split into two regions, North-Western and North-Eastern Rhodesia, which in 1911 were merged as Northern Rhodesia.

When it handed over the territory to the British Colonial Office on 1 April 1924, BSAC left in its wake an impoverished and underdeveloped country.

The colonial government set aside blocks of land for the exclusive use of Europeans and encouraged European immigration.

By 1930 thousands of Africans had been forced to move from prime land reserved for white settlers to less fertile land that quickly suffered degra-dation as a result of overcrowding. The hoped-for influx of white settlers did not happen and massive areas of fertile ground reverted to bush. Nevertheless, economic change was in the offing. Large copper deposits were found during the late 1920s just as the world was wiring up for electricity. The opening of several major mines and increased demand, especially during the Second World War, turned Northern Rhodesia into one of the world's top copper producers, with copper accounting for 90 per cent of the colony's exports.

But most of the profits were taken out of the country – notably to Britain and, after Federation, to Southern Rhodesia, where it was spent on infrastructure. Life remained bleak for the African population, despite its pivotal contribution to the economy.

Africans who flocked to the new towns and mines of the Copperbelt faced discrimination. A colour bar meant that they were prevented from being trained as skilled artisans and, compared to white workers, short-changed when it came to education and health facilities.

As a result, Zambia's nationalist politics was partly born down the mineshafts of the Copperbelt when miners fought to break down the colour bar and improve African pay and conditions. Most people, however, were influenced by the meetings held by and literature written by the leaders of the independence struggle, school teachers and clerks.

Zambia's first indigenous African political party was the Northern Rhodesia African National Congress. In response, the white settlers, led by Roy Welensky, pushed for closer ties with white counterparts in Southern Rhodesia and Nyasaland. In 1953 Northern Rhodesia, despite misgivings over the economic dominance of Southern Rhodesia and the opposition of its African population, joined Southern Rhodesia and Nyasaland to form the short-lived Central African Federation of Rhodesia and Nyasaland.

THE FIRST PRESIDENT

Nationalist resistance to the Federation grew as it became clear that the union was meant to protect the rights of whites to the detriment of Africans, with young politician Kenneth Kaunda (in picture) emerging as one of the nationalist leaders.

Through the early 1960s, nationalists continued to oppose colonial rule through a campaign of civil disobedience, code named Chachacha. The colonial government capitulated and under a complicated dual roll system election, in which every adult was allowed a vote, were held in October 1962. Neither Kaunda's United National Independence Party (UNIP) nor the African National Congress (ANC), led by Harry Nkumbula, were able to win a clear majority, so they formed a coalition government.

The Central African Federation was dissolved in 1963 and more elections were held in 1964, which were dominated by UNIP, and Kaunda became prime minister. Northern Rhodesia became independent on 24 October 1964, taking its name from the mighty Zambezi River that marked the new country's southern border.

Known simply as 'KK', Kaunda was faced with the challenge of building a country with very little resources. Zambia had little to show for its

DR. KENNETH KAUNDA

huge copper deposits with little infrastructure and poor health care outside of the line-of-rail between the Copperbelt and Livingstone. Human resource was also scarce, with just one hundred university graduates and a couple of thousand secondary school graduates in the country at independence.

Kaunda embarked on the difficult task of developing the country. He evolved a peculiar mix of Christian, Marxist and traditional African ideals known as 'humanism' in an effort to build a fair and classless society.

Riding high on a wave of post-independence optimism and enthusiasm, new schools, hospitals and factories were built, health and education services were provided free of charge, food prices were subsidized and hurried Zambianisation of public services was introduced.

The effect was a rapid decline in public services as newly promoted but under-trained Zambians struggled to cope. Food production slumped as farmers abandoned their fields for town jobs in the face of controlled prices for agricultural products and high-cost factories became a drain on government coffers. Political patronage, nepotism and corruption became widespread.

One year after independence, the new nation was hit badly by Southern Rhodesia's Unilateral Declaration of Independence (UDI) made in response to British plans for independence and black majority rule.

Southern Rhodesia was Zambia's most important trading partner and principal outlet for its copper. Out of solidarity for the black population, Kaunda immediately cut off all links. The country was forced to spend huge sums of money on communication links that bypassed Rhodesia and look north to Tanzania for alternative transport links to the outside world. By the time Zimbabwe gained its independence in 1980, the price of solidarity and sanctions had cost Zambia dearly.

Under the Mulungushi and Matero reforms of 1968 and 1969, the government nationalised the copper mines and other private enterprises. The timing could not have been worse. In the early 1970s, the bottom fell out of world copper prices, crippling Zambia's economy, while the price of the country's major import - oil, rocketed. The country fell further and further into debt and living standards of ordinary Zambians plummeted.

By the end of the decade Zambia's economy was in tatters. Inflation was rampant, the exchange rate was government controlled, foreign exchange was hard to obtain and corruption was widespread.

Biting poverty gradually formented opposition to the Kaunda one-party regime. After pressure from local interest groups and the donor community, the ban on opposition parties was lifted in July 1990. An opposition party, the Movement for Multi-Party Democracy or MMD emerged.

In a peaceful election in October 1991, the MMD led by trade unionist Frederick Chiluba was swept into power. To his credit, KK graciously conceded defeat and with Chiluba's presidential inauguration on 2 November 1991, Zambia became one of the first

LUSAKA BOMA (1928) NOW INDO-ZAMBIA BANK, CAIRO RD

African countries to make a smooth transition from one party to multi-party rule.

THE CHILUBA YEARS

DR. F. T. J. CHILUBA

Chiluba faced enormous economic troubles when he took over from Kaunda. Zambia was one of the poorest countries in the world, saddled with a US$7.3 billion debt burden, the equivalent of US$700 for every Zambian, and loss-making and bloated state-owned companies.

But the new president enjoyed the goodwill of the international community, which pumped billions of dollars of aid into the country in support of far-reaching market-based economic reforms.

The MMD removed all price and foreign exchange controls, freed interest rates, liberalised trade and set about privatizing parastatal companies. The economy picked up mar-ginally.

The social cost of the economic reforms was high. Thousands of jobs were slashed, especially in the mining sector which was also put up for sale, and the drift from the villages to the towns escalated, bringing with it problems of crime and rising levels of HIV/AIDS.

Zambia remained peaceful, no mean feat in a region beset by conflict, but Chiluba's credentials as a reformist democrat quickly took a battering.

MWANAWASA ERA

LEWY P. MWANAWASA, SC

On 27 December 2001 Zambians went to the polls, with a choice of 11 parties and presidential candidates. Mwanawasa was declared the winner, and sworn in on 2 January 2002.

E. KOLLENBERG & SON

CAIRO RD 1929

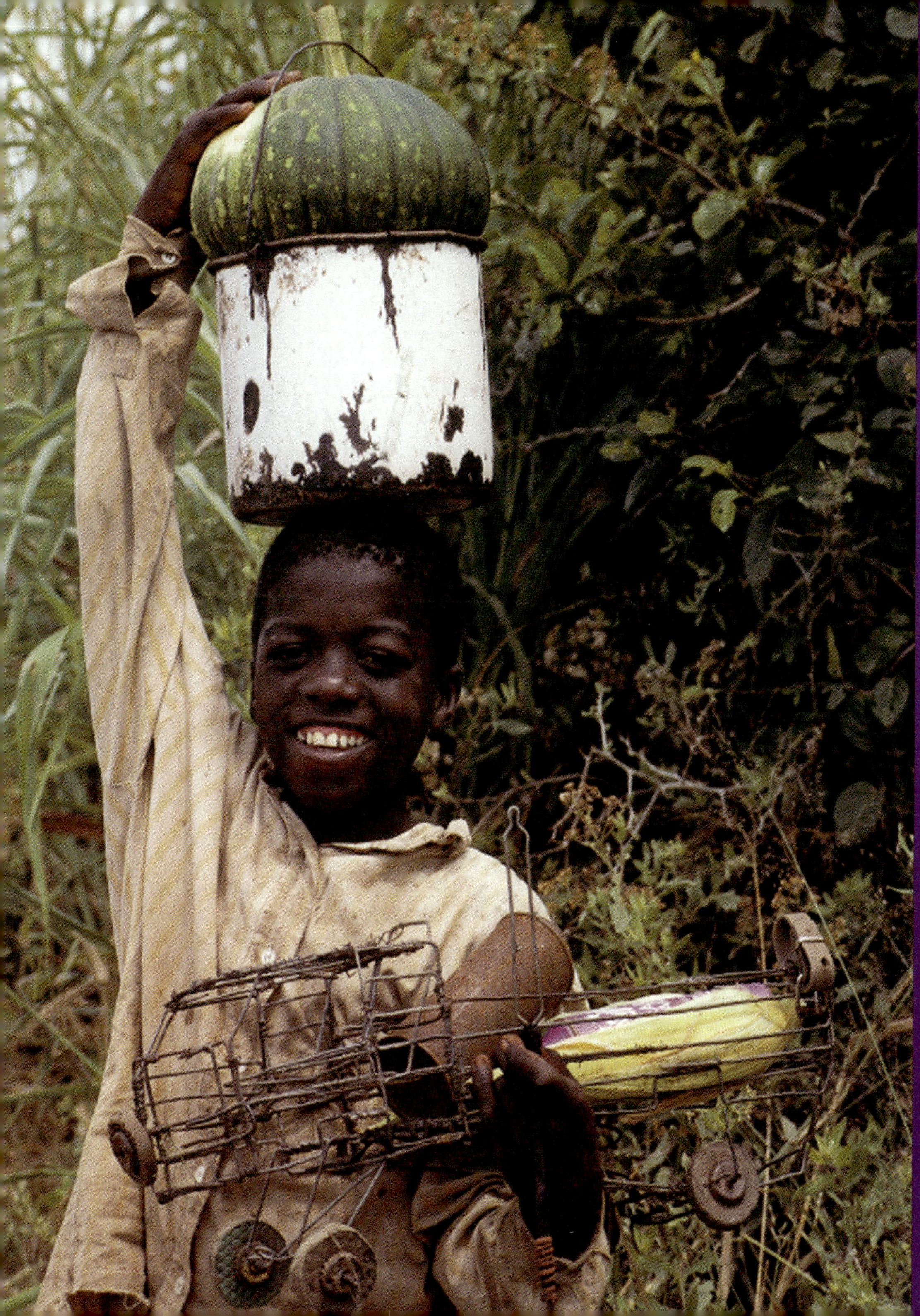

One of the most bizarrely shaped African countries, Zambia covers about 750,00 square kilometres (290,000 square miles). It is landlocked and part of the Southern Central African plateau.

The country's altitude, much of which is between 1,060 and 1,363 meters (3,500 and 4,500 feet) above sea level, means temperatures and humidity are bearable in most places at most times of the year, although it certainly feels like the tropics in lower areas such as the Zambezi and Luangwa Valleys.

Broken by isolated ridges rising to more than 2,150 meters (7,000 feet), the country is covered mainly by deciduous woodland, with areas of tropical grasslands and wetlands.

In the east and south, Zambia is sliced by deep valleys, branches of the Great Rift Valley, the gigantic fault in the earth's surface that runs down most of the length of the eastern side of Africa. The largest, the Zambezi Valley, forms the country's southern border with Zimbabwe, while the 700 km long Luangwa Valley is lined by the steep and spectacular Muchinga Escarpment. Much of the west of Zambia is a gigantic flood plain, the Kafue Flats, with endless rolling grasslands, where Africa's second largest wildebeest migration takes place.

Several remarkable rivers flow through the country: the mighty Zambezi, Kafue, and Luangwa; and in the north, the Chambeshi and Luapula.

Zambia's most famous waterfall is the magnificent Victoria Falls, or Mosi-o-Tunya, the largest waterfall in the world, where the Zambezi plunges over a mile-wide cliff and thunders down the long zig-zagging Batoka Gorge.

'The Smoke that Thunders' is not the only impressive waterfall in Zambia, which has a huge number of cascades, especially in the north.

Northern Zambia also boasts the massive Lake

Tanganyika, the second deepest in the world and awash with colourful cichlid fish.

Zambia is divided into nine administrative provinces: Northern, North-Western, Copperbelt, Luapula, Eastern, Western, Central, Lusaka and Southern.

THE PEOPLE

The Zambian government officially recognises 73 different tribes or ethnic groups, all of which speak Bantu languages. Each of these tribes has its own cultural identity, including language and social systems, and its own traditional territory. Many are reviving centuries-old ceremonies (see Traditonal ceremonies, page 34)

Although Zambians are proud of their tribal origins, there is little tension between different groups and intermarriages between tribes are common.

The larger tribes include the Bemba, who make up the largest tribal group at 20 per cent of Zambia's 10 million population. Their traditional homeland is in northern Zambia, a large area around the town of Kasama. Originally from what is now Democratic Republic of Congo, many migrated to the Copperbelt, where Bemba is now the *lingua franca*.

The Tonga people come from the south of the country, including the Zambezi Valley, and make up 15 per cent of Zambia's people. The Chewa people are found in Eastern Province, around the town of Chipata. They comprise one third of the country's 1.5 million Nyanja-speakers.

Other Nyanja-speakers are the Ngonis, who also live in the east of the country and are descended from the Zulus who migrated here in the early nineteenth century. The Nsenga people are also Nyanja-speaking. They make up about 5 per cent of the population and live close to the town of Petauke and along the lower Luangwa River.

Lozi-speakers, who number about 600,000 people, come from the west of Zambia, and form their own distinct identity in a part of Zambia known as Barotseland. Life revolves around the waters of the vast Zambezi flood plain.

The non-African population includes Europeans, Asians mainly from India and those of mixed descent.

RELIGION

Zambia was declared a Christian nation, although the right to religious freedom is guaranteed under the constitution.

Religion plays a central part in the lives of most Zambians and church attendance is high. There are many Christian denominations including Anglican, Baptist, Evangelical, Jehovah Witnesses, Roman Catholic and Seventh Day Adventist.

There are also Hindu, Muslim, Jewish and Sikh communities based almost exclusively in the urban areas and even smaller communities of Bahais and Buddhists.

Most traditional religions, which are strong in rural areas, are animist. They revolve around a belief in natural objects possessing life and consciousness of a Supreme Being and give a lot of importance to ancestors, whose main

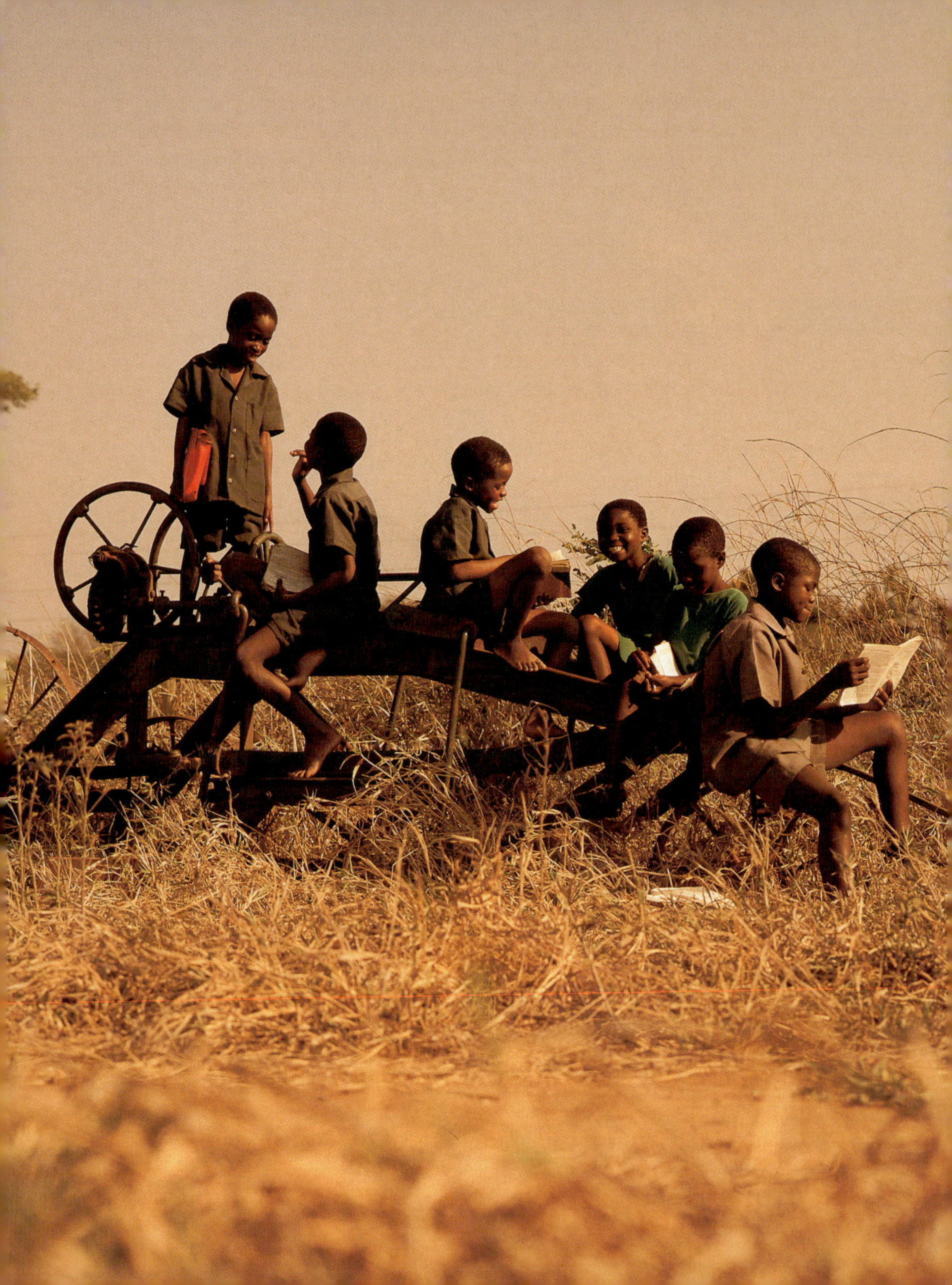

role is to protect the people. Townspeople tend to move away from village beliefs, partly because their way of life changes, but nevertheless ceremonies in the range of independent African churches combine Christianity and traditional beliefs.

GOVERNMENT

Zambia has a British-style parliamentary democracy. Government consists of the president and the 158-seat national assembly.

Elections are held every five years and the presidency is limited to two five-years terms. There are also traditional chiefs and their headmen, who still command a great deal of respect but hold little decision-making power except when it comes to land distribution.

ECONOMY

Despite years of decline, the now privatised copper mining industry is Zambia's main source of income bringing in about 65 per cent of foreign exchange earnings from exports.

Zambia also has substantial deposits of many other minerals, principally cobalt (a by product of copper mining), coal, zinc, lead, gold, silver, limestone, uranium and manganese. Emeralds, amethysts, garnets, tourmalines and other semi-precious stones are also mined. Zambia's domestic economy is based on agriculture. Maize is the staple food. Other crops grown are tobacco, cassava, wheat, millet, vegetables, sugar cane, groundnuts, sweet potatoes, fruits, sorghum and soya beans. The commercial farm sector is growing, and now accounts for close to half agricultural output, much of this is for export, including flowers and vegetables, such as baby corn and mangetout. Tobacco, coffee, sugar cane, cotton and tea are also export crops.

The economy remains dependent on foreign aid and loans from the international financial institutions. Tourism is a growing industry.

SOCIAL CONVENTIONS

Zambia is a peaceful and safe country, with friendly people and spectacular scenery and wildlife.

Greetings are accorded considerable importance in Zambia. This generally means a conventional handshake followed by a few polite enquiries about the family and life in general. Don't be surprised if the handshake is followed by a cross grip of your thumb and finished off with a repeat of the handshake. During this greeting, many people also use the left hand to support their right arm.

In rural areas greetings are much more formal and stylish than in the west. They can be very complex and are often dictated by the sex, age and relationship to the individual. Verbal greetings are often accompanied by handshakes and handclaps. As a mark of respect people will often bob or kneel, especially when greeting elders. As a visitor these types of greetings will not be expected of you. In the rural areas people, particularly children, will give you a friendly wave even if they don't know you. Wave back or even wave first.

NGONI WEDDING

If you are walking in the more remote areas it is also customary to greet anyone you meet.

Don't be offended by hissing, as this is a common way of attracting the attention of someone who is far away. Displays of intimacy in public should be avoided. Zambians are also fairly formal in their forms of address. Although many will use first names when speaking to people of their age or younger, bear in mind that it is considered disrespectful to call elders by their first name. As a visitor if you are meeting someone for the first time, unless they happen to be young, always address him or her as 'Mr or Mrs so-and-so'.

People also call each other daddy, mummy, uncle, aunty, brother, sister, madam or boss, all regarded as respectful and perfectly acceptable if you don't know someone's name. Most travellers will experience warmth and hospitality and if you're invited into a Zambian home a few small items presented as gifts will be much appreciated. Soft drinks, tea, sugar and other basic goods are acceptable.

Also well received are souvenirs from your country. Be sensitive, however. Poverty levels in Zambia are very high and while you may sometimes find such poverty distressing, resist the temptation to hand out money, clothes and sweets. Instead, you could get in contact with one of the numerous charities and development agencies.

Some lodges in national parks have started funding various social projects, especially schools, so ask if you can make a contribution. Although rural poverty is more widespread than in urban areas, it is in the cities and towns where you are likely to encounter street children and beggars. Bear in mind that people are often late for appointments and transport may not leave at the scheduled time. So don't be too rigid when it comes to time-keeping. Zambians are always delighted when you make an effort to follow their customs, even in urban areas where culture is greatly influenced by contemporary American and European culture.

SHIMUNENGA

TRADITIONAL CEREMONIES

The numerous ethnic groups of Zambia pride themselves on a variety of colourful and captivating traditional ceremonies, many of which are rarely seen by visitors. Many festivals were discouraged by the colonial authorities, which saw them as a threat, or simply forgotten as people moved from villages to the towns.

Several of these festivals were revived in the 1970s and 1980s, encouraged by Zambia's first president, Kenneth Kaunda, who wanted people to be aware of their cultural origins.

In theory, there are now over 20 festivals held all over the country every year. In reality, many are small events, which may not take place each year and are in remote parts of the country, difficult for visitors to access.

Contact the Zambia National Tourist Board on tel 01 229087-90, or the Department of Cultural Services on tel 01 223902/9. Keep a lookout for announcements on local TV, newspapers or through travel agents on how to get there, where to stay and the exact dates of festivals. If you manage to get to a ceremony, you will discover that they are genuine affairs, where rituals are performed for the benefit of the local people not the odd tourist watching.

It's worth finding a guide or asking local people to explain the significance of the rituals and how you should behave. Some of the ceremonies, notably the Lozi's Kuomboka, follow a strict protocol and tourists are not spared the whip, literally sometimes, if they step out of line.

Although the many festivals have different origins and significance, some have similar features and themes. Drumming, music and dancing, often in traditional and brightly coloured ceremonial costumes, are central parts of most festivals.

One of Zambia's most popular dance forms at festi-

THE LITUNGA OF THE LOZI- KUOMBOKA CEREMONY

FLOOD PLAINS- KUOMBOKA CEREMONY

vals is called the Makishi, performed by troupes of energetic dancers wearing brightly coloured skirts and leg tassels, with equally colourful face masks surrounded by a mane of feathers or grass. Makishi originated in the west of Zambia but is now performed all over the country, which illustrates the vitality of ceremonies.

Speeches, singing and recitals designed to remind people about the history and legends of the tribe are also key components of most festivals, as is heavy drinking.

Many festivals are also occasions for young boys and girls who have just been through initiation into adulthood to be presented to the tribe.

KUOMBOKA

The Kuomboka (which means to 'move to dry ground') is the biggest and most famous of Zambia's ceremonies. It is celebrated by the Lozi people of Western Province living in the floodplains of the Upper Zambezi. The event marks the journey of their king, the Litunga, as the swollen Zambezi River temporarily floods his winter palace at Lealui, about 15km west of the town of Mongu, to dry ground.

Although Kuomboka was already a long-standing tradition, it was Litunga Yeta III who in 1933 first made the move from the winter palace at Lealui to the summer Limulunga Palace the major and colourful ceremony it is today. He built a palace on permanently dry land at Limulunga. The Litunga's departure is heralded by the beating of three huge old royal war drums – mundili, munanga and kanaona, each more than 1 metre wide and said to be about 170 years old.

At the heart of the ceremony is the Nalikwanda, a black-and-white striped royal barge topped with a carved elephant. When a Litunga dies, his barge is supposed to be sunk and a new one built for his successor – but in recent years the same barge has been used for two Litunga due to financial constraints.

In a journey lasting about six hours, to the accompaniment of pulsating drums and xylophones, the Litunga is paddled through a series of canals across the lush greenery of the floodplain by over a hundred men, who each wear a headdress of a scarlet beret with a piece of lion's mane and a knee-length skirt of animal skins. As the barge moves off into the distance, all one can see is an elephant slowly bobbing its way through the grass.

The Litunga's Queen, the Moyo, follows in a smaller but no less impressive barge surrounded by a flotilla of smaller canoes.

An advance party of 'scout' canoes announces the imminent arrival of the Litunga at Limulunga, at the same time delighting the thousands waiting on the river banks by using their paddles to spray water. By the time he arrives, the Litunga has changed from traditional dress into, bizarrely, the uniform of a nineteenth century British ambassador, complete with regalia and ostrich-plumed hat. This was first presented to the Litunga in 1902 by the British King, Edward VII, in recognition of treaties

THE NALIKWANDA, KUOMBOKA CEREMONY

signed between the Lozi, who lived in Barotseland which then had the unusual status of being a protectorate within Northern Rhodesia, and Queen Victoria. The agreement signed in 1900 between Litunga Lewanika and Cecil Rhodes and his British South Africa Company gave the Kingdom of Barotseland a semblance of independence within Northern Rhodesia. At its peak, the Kingdom comprised much of the upper Zambezi basin stretching from the Victoria Falls to the Caprivi Strip of modern-day Namibia.

The Lozi organised a highly sophisticated labour-intensive economic and political system to exploit the Zambezi floodplain, which involved building villages on mounds, constructing canals and developing different skills and products throughout the kingdom.

Barotseland's independence was not recognised when Zambia broke away from the colonial power. This remains a sore point and there are still occasional calls for the secession of the Kingdom from Zambia by some Lozi.

At the safe arrival of their ruler, the crowd roars with delight and relief and immediately surrounds him as he walks the remaining few hundred yards to his palace.

Be careful at this stage, because it quickly becomes a crush - and tourist or no tourist, the Litunga's bodyguards are quite prepared to whip anyone who gets too close. Women should also note that standing too close, especially with their back turned to the royal barge and the Litunga sends a hiss of disapproval through the crowd. Menstruating women are considered to bring bad luck to the royal household, so banning all women gets round the sticky problem of finding out who's in their cycle and who's not.

The precise date of the retreat from the rising water to higher ground is only known a week or so in advance, and announced on local TV and the press. Now that Kuomboka attracts more visitors it is usually held around Easter time, close to the full moon. But check beforehand - if water levels are not high enough, it will not be held at all. In fact, if you are an overseas visitor with limited time, you may, wisely, decide this is too unpredictable.

The return journey, the Kufuhela, which means to go down, is a comparatively low key but no less interesting affair. For details on how to get there and where to stay see Mongu section on page 178.

UMUTOMBOKO

The spectacular and colourful Umutomboko ceremony is held every year over two days, usually on the last weekend of July, by the Lunda people of Luapula. The festival celebrates their migration from present day Democratic Republic of Congo or 'crossing of the river', and military victories over other tribes.

Umutomboko is held in Luapula Province at a village called Mwansabombwe, between the town of Mwense and Lake Mweru and at the site of the Lunda royal capital founded in 1890 by Mwata Kazembe Kanyembo Ntemena.

MWATA KAZEMBE - UMTOMBOKA

The ceremony begins with the paramount chief, Mwata Kazembe, performing traditional rituals at a number of sacred places within and outside the royal palace. Visitors and in fact most Lunda people do not have the privilege of being privy to this occasion as it is restricted to the Mwata and a few of his dignitaries.

Then, covered in white powder, the Mwata receives tributes of food and drink from his subjects, which leads to much feasting and celebration. On the second day, an animal is slaughtered and Mwata Kazembe, dressed in a zebra skin known as muselo, is borne by eight men to a central arena. He is surrounded by hundreds of his subjects, cheering, drumming, dancing and letting off gun volleys.

Here he performs the Mutomboko, the Lunda dance of victory and climax of the ceremony. The battles are long over but the dance goes on, led magnificently by the Mwata Kazembe. Armed with a sword and an axe, he is dressed in the mukonzo, a heavy skirt-like garment, made of over forty meters of cloth gathered into thick folds around the waist.

Trailing from the mukonzo is another piece of cloth, called the lucaca, which is held by an attendant, who must keep time with the dancing of Mwata Kazembe.

As he dances, the Mwata Kazembe points his sword to the north, east, south and west, then to the sky and to the earth indicating that only God and death can conquer him. The ceremony comes to an end when the chief is carried back to his palace.

The Lunda tribe broke away from the Lunda state of the Mwata Yamvo in the Democratic Republic of Congo in the late seventeenth century, settling in the fertile Luapula valley.

At first they remained loyal to Mwata Yamvo but by the mid-eighteenth century Kazembe's Lunda eclipsed the parent power and dominated trade routes and much of the political life in Southern Democratic Republic of Congo and north-eastern Zambia.

The Kingdom fell into decline in the mid-nineteenth century and was stripped off much of its power with the coming of colonialism.

LIKUMBI LYA MIZE

Likumbi Lya Mize is a celebration of the culture of the Luvale people who live in the far west of Zambia, near the town of Zambezi.

The festival, which is named the Day of Mize after the early Luvale capital, usually happens over several days in July or August and is an ideal opportunity to see Zambia's famed Makishi dancers.

The Makishi (the singular is Likishi) are masked characters, each with its own distinctive dancing styles, from the graceful to the funny and acrobatic. Most characters are from Luvale mythology but some are based on modern day situations.

Examples include Munguli the hyena, Ngaji, an elegant dancer who, with his beautifully woven costume, is considered to be the most beautiful of all the Makishi. There is also Likishi Lya Mwana-

MASKED LIKISHI- LIKUMBI LYA MIZE

Pwebo, a crowd puller and perhaps the best known Likishi. Dressed like a girl, he dances on a string tied between two poles.

It is believed that as he is dancing on the string the spirit of his wife is with him. That is why a dancer's wife will never look up at her husband performing the dance. Only once he is safely back on the ground will she go to meet her husband, at which point her spirit is thought to return to her.

All Makishi are dressed in flamboyant masks and costumes, which show off the unique Luvale skill and tradition of intricate mask-making. Women and children are told by their menfolk that the makishi are in fact from the world of the dead.

Praise singers reciting the history of the tribe and the Luvale royalty offer the Luvale a chance to reaffirm social ties and their loyalty to the tribe's paramount chief.

The people get a rare opportunity to catch a glimpse of their chief, who is elaborately clad in colourful robes, wearing his Muchama crown and carrying a fly whisk. The Luvale are one of the peoples who migrated from the Democratic Republic of Congo.

Traditionally, they were fishermen and hunters but also, they became one of the first Zambian people to establish trade links with non-Africans. By the eighteenth century, they were trading with Portuguese and Brazilian traders to the west in Angola.

LIKUMBI LYA MIZE

INITIATION OF GIRLS TO PUBERTY - FEATURE OF MOST TRADITIONAL CEREMONIES

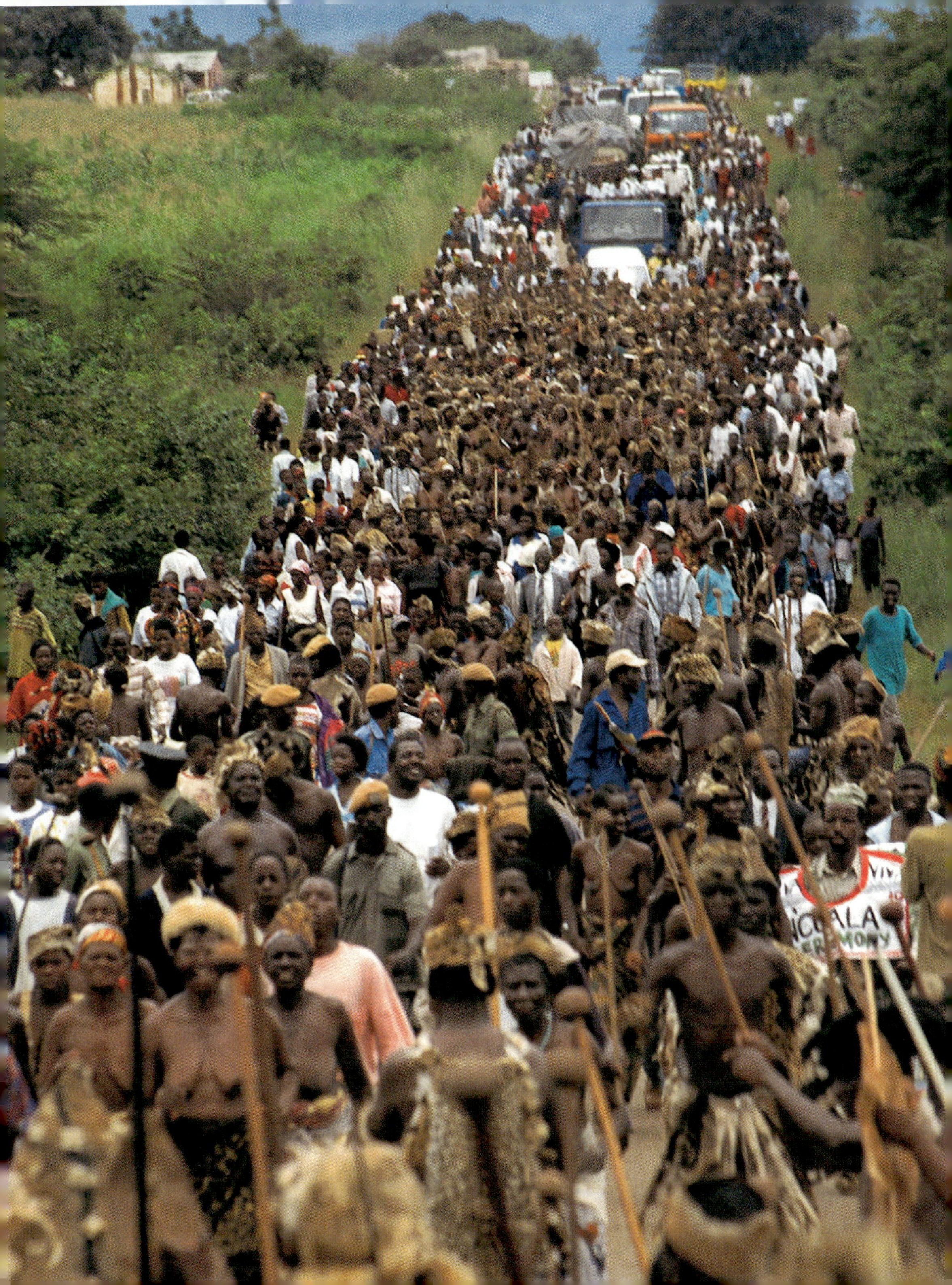

NGONI WARRIORS- NC'WALA CEREMONY

NC'WALA

Nc'wala celebrates the first fruits of a new harvest. It is perhaps the most dramatic of several harvest festivals. Thousands of colourfully dressed Ngoni people gather at Mutenguleni village, a few kilometres from Chipata in Eastern Province, usually at the end of February to mark the end of a successful rainy season and the beginning of a good harvest. The Nc'wala is one of the festivals recently revived after an absence of 80 years. The first ritual involves the chief tasting the first fresh produce of the year amid much singing and dancing. His ritual rebirth includes his being locked up in his house and drinking a cup of blood from a black bull, stabbed to death by a spear. An offshoot of the Zulus of South Africa, the Ngoni's military prowess is also shown off in the Nc'wala. This includes displays of the Ngoni war dance performed by leopard skin clad warriors, complete with shields and knobkerries. Among the tribes in Zambia, the Ngoni can be said to have made the most spectacular entry in the country. On the day they crossed the Zambezi from the south, 20th November 1835, there was a total eclipse of the sun.

SHIMUNENGA

The Ila people, who are closely related to the Tonga of southern Zambia, celebrate the Shimunenga on the weekend of a full moon in September or October at Maal on the Kafue Flats about 40km west of Namwala. The ceremony used to be a hunt of lechwe but now involves driving cattle across the Kafue River and signifies an episode in the tribe's history when the younger brother of a chief called Shimunenga broke away to form his own clan. An angry Shiumunenga defeated the breakaway army and banished his brother, forcing him to cross a river marking the edge of his land. But before the brother could cross, he died, which was interpreted as a sign from the ancestors, whose spirits lived in the waters, that they needed to unite. Offerings are made to the ancestors in the river, there are mock fights, singing, dancing and drinking.

ILA WARRIORS - SHIMUNENGA CEREMONY

SYMBOLIC CHASING OF COWS- SHIMUNENGE

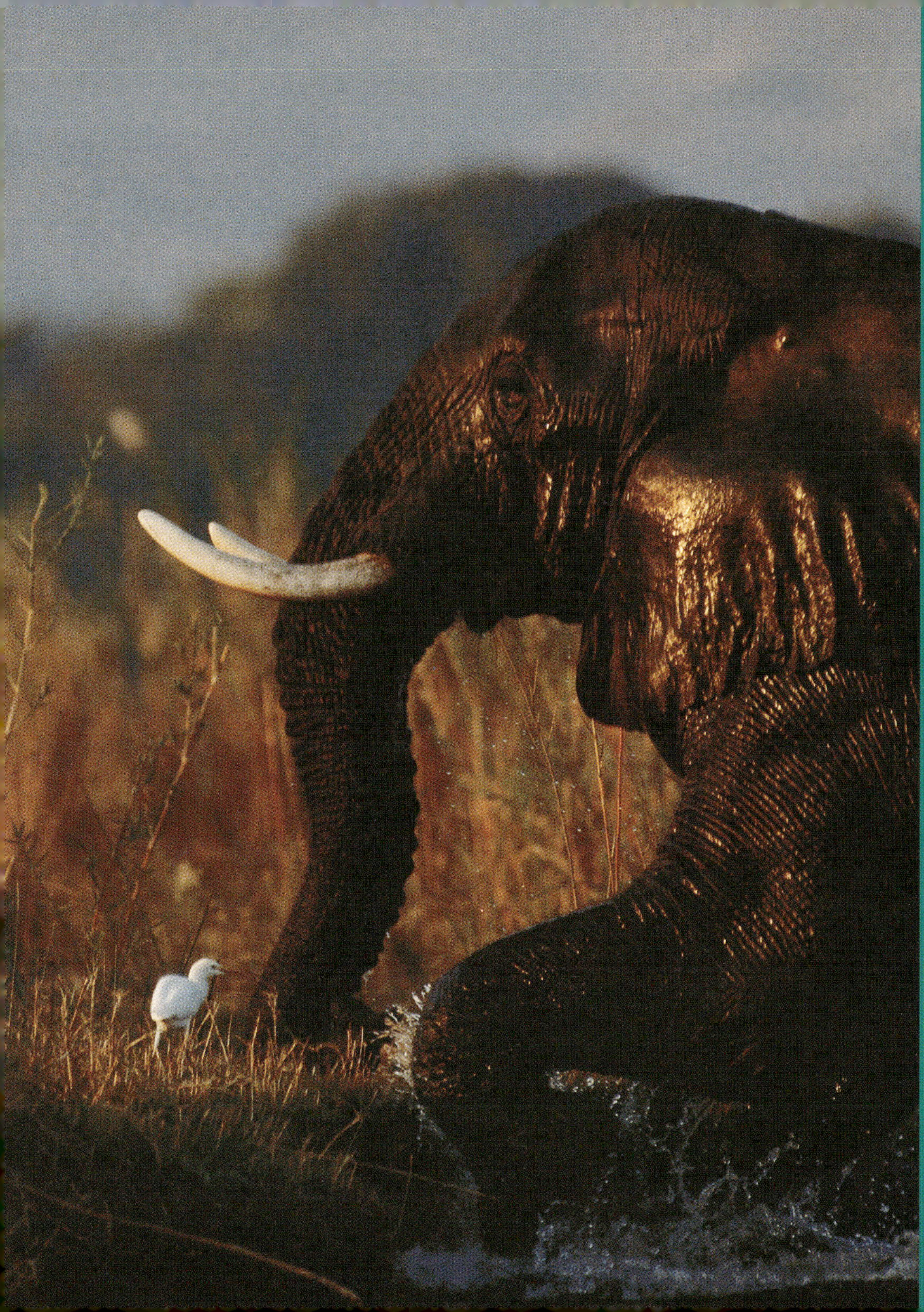

NATIONAL PARKS

Covering about 30 per cent of the country, Zambia's parks are unspoiled and far wilder than others elsewhere in Africa. Zambia is famous as the birthplace of the walking safari and although numbers are growing, it is still unusual to find hordes of tourists in the game parks, and sometimes it really is just you, the safari guide and the animals. There are 19 national parks and 34 game management areas, which are administered by the government agency Zambia Wildlife Authority (ZAWA). There are a number of parks with good tourist facilities where visitors can come face-to-face with large numbers of different animals, including sub-species unique to Zambia such as Cookson's wildebeest and Thornicroft's giraffe.

Lack of infrastructure make many of the parks inaccessible and poaching has decimated animal numbers where there is little control. The high-profile parks are: South Luangwa in eastern Zambia, the Kafue in the west, Mosi-o-Tunya, and Lower Zambezi in the south. A visit is also highly recommended to the small and beautiful Kasanka National Park, famous for its straw-coloured fruit bats, which gather in their millions in November and December, and the shy, rare swamp-dwelling sitatunga.

ANIMAL WATCHING

Plenty of wildlife and few visitors mean Zambia is one of the most exciting and overlooked safari destinations in Africa.

Zambia is home to the classic African animals – elephant, lion, leopard, cheetah, giraffe, zebra, buffalo, hippo – as well as more unusual and endangered species including the African wild dog with its large round ears, long legs and patchy black, yellow and white colouring, and one of the rarest African birds, the strange-looking and elusive shoebill stork, found only in a few spots including Zambia's Bangweulu Wetlands.

You'll see large herds of buffalo, antelope, including impala, puku and lechwe. Africa's most endangered animal the black rhino, which was wiped out by poaching in the 1970's and 1980's has been reintroduced to North Luangwa National Park. There are a handful of white rhinos in the Mosi-o-Tunya near Victoria Falls. Other animals you may see in the parks include hyena, genet, civet, serval cats, mongoose, vervet monkeys, baboon and crocodile.

Over 750 species of birds, including the rare wattled crane, fish eagles, bee-eaters and sunbirds, make Zambia, especially the north and the west, a must-see country for serious birdwatchers. There is also an abundance of butterfly, insect and plant species.

How to get there

Zambia has a number of experienced safari operators (see pages 78-83) who are able to plan a trip for you. They will arrange everything including flights, accommodation and game drives. However, if you have your own 4WD vehicle and wish to explore some of the less visited parks you will need to plan the trip with great care and carry along all your equipment. It pays to seek advice from lodge owners and local residents on journey times and road conditions.

Where to stay

Lodges and tented camps are the most common type of accommodation in the parks. Most lodges nowadays have been designed to blend into the surrounding environment, often built of stone and timber with thatched roofs. Among the best in Africa, lodges usually cater for a small number of people, offering a high standard of food and attentive service, with staff often outnumbering clients and matching high prices. In many ways, the tented camp offers visitors the quintessential African safari experience.

A tented camp can be anything from spacious, twin-bedded, walk-in tents, equipped with every conceivable creature comfort, from ensuite bathrooms to double beds, to the more practical, but still comfortable tents used on mobile safaris.

Accommodation in the more popular parks is usually booked well in advance, especially at peak periods, so always make your reservations early.

Many establishments may not accept very young children so always make inquiries concerning any age restrictions. In the undeveloped parks there are no facilities of any kind so you'll have to be prepared to camp and bring all your own equipment, including food and water.

When to go

The amount of wildlife you see will depend on the season in which you visit. As a general rule, you will see more animals during the dry season (April to November) because they tend to concentrate near water holes and are not hidden by the long grass. Birdwatching is best in the rainy season, especially November and December.

GAME VIEWING TIPS

To get as much as possible out of your visit, consider as essential equipment a camera with a very powerful telescopic lens, a good pair of binoculars and a good reference book describing the wildlife you are likely to see.

Nearly all lodges and camps have their own vehicles and run regular game drives during the day and night. Going along with a guide who knows the animals and area is the best way to see a park. Make the most of these trips by asking questions and telling the guide of any special interests you may have. It is worth going on at least two game drives - one during the day, either morning or afternoon and the other at night to widen the chances of seeing as many different animals as possible. Once in the park don't expect to see large herds of animals round every corner. Instead take time to also enjoy the beauty and smells of the bush, including the birds, insects, plants and expanses of water glistening in the sun. Please do not disregard the parks' rules and guidelines - they are there to protect a fragile, diminishing wilderness and for your safety. Always keep a good distance from all the animals and take note of what's happening around you.

Do not talk loudly or try to attract the attention of animals by making noise - they are perfectly aware of your presence.

Never under any circumstances feed any of the animals.

Never get out of your vehicle unless you are on a walking safari, which should only be done under the guidance of an expert guide. Always obey the guide's instructions. Wildlife is unpredictable and the guide's instructions are intended to make your experience as enjoyable and safe as possible.

Driving

Venturing into the park by yourself will require a sturdy and reliable four-wheel drive, sound driving experience and careful planning. If you are going in for a day trip, make sure you are out of the park by twilight.

For longer trips, it's always wise to travel with another vehicle in case of an emergency and ensure you carry everything you're likely to need with you. The following should be considered as essential:

tow-rope	radiator hoses
torch	high pressure hoses
shovel	fire extinguisher
winch	good set of tools
fan belt	two spare wheels
vehicle fluids	puncture repair kit
points	pump
fuel pump	jack

Ensure the spare wheels are bolted firmly onto the vehicle and your vehicle has a sturdy roof rack that will not collapse under the weight of your load. An additional fuel tank is an added bonus. Remember that bumpy roads can damage or break equipment, so ensure all equipment is strapped down and protected from dust by thick tarpaulin. Make sure you carry enough water, food, fuel, camping equipment, spare wheels

ZAMBIAN
National Parks and
Game Management Areas

Game Managment Areas

National Parks

Towns

Mweru Wantipa

Sumbu

Lusenga Plain

Nyika

Isangano

North Luangwa

Luambe

Lukusuzi

CHIPATA

Lavushi

Kasanka

South Luangwa

Lower Zambezi

Chimfunshi
Chimpanzee
Sanctuary

KITWE

West Lunga

LUSAKA

Blue
Lagoon

Lochinvar

LIVINGSTONE

Kafue

Liuwa Plains

Sioma
Ngwezi

Mosi-oa-Tunya

PETER JONES ©

and tools. Carry at least six litres of water per person per day and at least 20 litres of extra fuel in a jerry can.

Camping equipment should include sleeping bags, tents, fold-up chairs and tables, and cooking implements, including matches and a tin opener. Before visiting any of the national parks off the tourist circuit it's advisable to visit the nearest ZAWA office to inform them of your plans and to get the latest advice about conditions in the park. For the really remote and seldom visited parks, it may be wise to ask an experienced guide to travel with you. Carry a map, compass and global positioning system (GPS) to help keep you on the right path.

Make a note of landmarks and when asking directions remember your concept of distances and time is different from most Zambians. Once in the park, protect the environment by sticking to roads and tracks unless there's an emergency. If you have to drive through long grass bear in mind that it collects under the vehicle and the seeds it scatters can block the radiator causing the engine to overheat. Fix a net to the front of the radiator grille to block the grass seeds and insects and stop regularly to remove as much grass from under the vehicle as possible. In some game parks during the rainy season, roads become impassable while others such as South Luangwa have all-weather roads. Check with parks and lodge operators.

HUNTING

Visitors to Zambia can hunt only as part of a licensed trip organised by a recognised safari hunting company. Safari hunting is carefully controlled and is permitted in game management areas, i.e. the buffer areas surrounding Zambia's national parks. Always check for the latest information on hunting procedures. Communities living in game management areas are allowed to use wildlife as a resource and are realising some benefits from highly lucrative hunting safaris. Some of the hunting revenue is pumped back into communities in the form of schools, clinics, grinding mills and other infrastructure. Contact: Zambia Wildlife Authority (ZAWA), tel: 01 278366, fax: 01 278244 email: zawaorg@zamnet.zm.

SAFARI

A typical safari day starts with an early tea or coffee and light breakfast around the campfire watching the sun rise, followed by a four-hour drive tracking animals during which there's time to stop for a drink, a bite to eat and chance to soak up some of the most stunning scenery and smells of the bush in the world. Back at camp, you'll be treated to an enormous and delicious brunch after which most guests, understandably, go for a siesta or just relax before the afternoon's game drive. Highlights of night drives, which again last on average four hours, are the stop for sundowner drinks and nibbles and tracking of nocturnal animals, including the elusive leopard, with a spotlight. It's worth doing both day and night drives because of the different animals you'll encounter. Both are exhilarating in their own ways, as are the other alternative to drives: for example, Luangwa Valley's world-famous and highly regarded walking safaris and canoe safaris.

For walking safaris, you can go the whole hog and do a few days of walking from bushcamp to bushcamp, not as basic as their name suggests but comfortable and in some cases very luxurious. There's nothing quite like the thrilling experience of coming face-to-face with wildlife, all under the guard of an armed and trained scout. Walking safaris allow a fuller experience of the African bush, including the smaller creatures, the plants and animal tracks.

Dedicated walking safaris are exclusive upmarket affairs - you'll be looking at US$300 per person per day. The main operators include the Bushcamps Company, Norman Carr Safaris (the founder of the walking safari), Robin Pope Safaris and Remote Africa Safaris. Alternatively, you can organise an afternoon or morning walk from your camp. For popular canoe safaris, try the wonderful Lower Zambezi. Canoe safaris combine exhilaration and relaxation as you alternatively paddle and drift downstream with the current, enjoying the sights and sounds of the river from the river. From a few meters away, it is possible to watch herds of buffalo coming down to drink, elephants swimming across and, of course, the busy birds, nesting or fishing. Trips are usually not too arduous and last between three and five days, athough some companies are planning to introduce trips which involve more canoeing and less wildlife viewing on more appropriate river stretches. All budgets are catered for: budget travellers sleep in tents, sometimes on midstream sandbank, while the more well-heeled get the luxury of a permanent camp with fine food and wine.

The best section of the Lower Zambezi River for seeing animals is the stretch between the Chongwe River which passes through the Lower Zambezi National Park as far as the confluence with the Luangwa, taking in the spectacular Mpata Gorge. The few specialist operators include Kiboko Adventures, Safari Par Excellence, Sobek Zambezi Adventures and Shenton Safaris. For more details, see chapters which include different parks and their particular attractions.

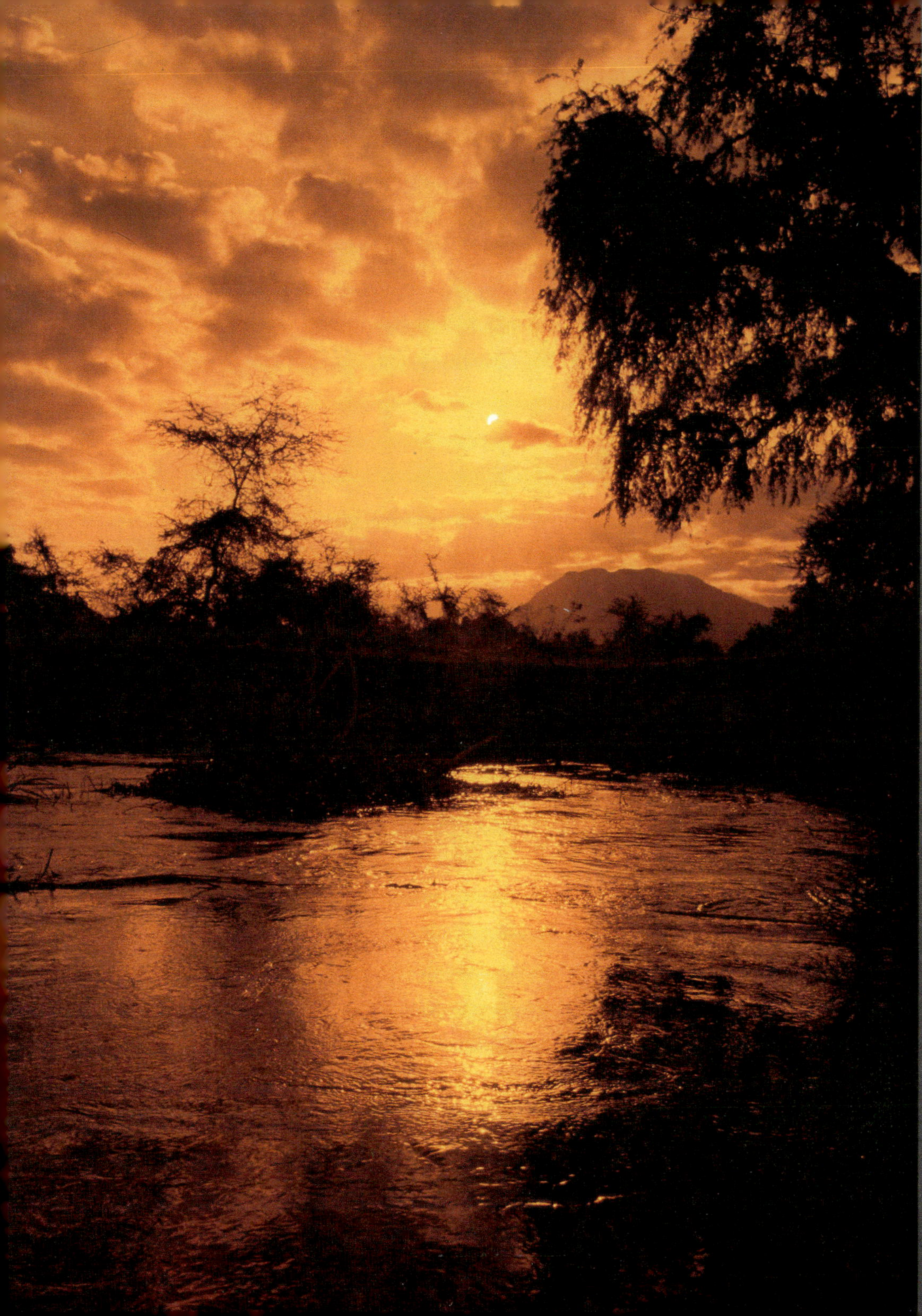

Entertainment

A night out in Zambia usually means eating, drinking and dancing. In the bigger cities, the range of restaurants, bars and nightclubs is more extensive, and, although choices are limited, it is possible to take in a play, film or live band, especially in Lusaka.

Major towns have good sporting facilities and there is always a football match to watch. See individual relevant chapters for more details of recommended places.

shopping

There are a number of well-stocked supermarkets, shopping complexes and food markets in major cities as well as some impressive craft markets where bargaining is acceptable. See individual relevant chapters for more details of recommended places.

Business hours

Banking hours are 08:15 -15:00, Monday to Friday and on the last Saturday of every month. Government offices are usually open between 08:00 to 13:00 and 14:00 to 17:00, Monday to Friday.

Private offices tend to keep the same hours but are open over lunchtime and usually on Saturday mornings. Shop hours vary between 08:00 and 09:00 to 16:30 and 17:30, Monday to Friday, although some of the supermarkets stay open until 20:00. Saturday is a working day and some shops also open for some hours on Sunday.

Art and Craft

Overshadowed for years by the richer traditions of neighbouring Zimbabwe and Democratic Republic of Congo (former Zaire), Zambia's arts scene is starting to come into its own.

Most months in Lusaka and Livingstone there are art exhibitions showcasing the work of a small group of local contemporary painters, sculptors and ceramic artists, some of whom have studied abroad and often blend Western with traditional styles. Pieces often depict Zambia's social, economic and political concerns and can be purchased at the handful of private galleries mostly found in the capital. Look out for Flinto Chandia, Lutanda, Mulenga Chafilwa, Vandita, Laurey Nevers, Friday Tembo and Patrick Mumba's works.

Craft centres, urban and rural markets and roadside stalls boast a variety of local handicrafts, including traditional musical instruments, items made from wire and brightly-coloured *chitenge* cloth, copperware, households items such as spoons, bowls, stools, mats, wood and cane furniture, carvings of elephants, hippos, giraffes made from wood and soapstone.

Zambian basketwork, especially from the Western and Southern Provinces, can be very beautiful and intricate. Local people especially in villages continue to use the baskets for their traditional purposes, such as carrying food or trapping fish. Tourists can buy some wonderful works, for example on the roadside to Siavonga, as souvenirs for back home.

Equally impressive are Zambia's traditional clay pots, which come in a variety of simple shapes and sizes and are shaped by hand using no artificial colours.

More expensive items include handcrafted silver jewellery inset with semi-precious gemstones.

Art is not limited to galleries and drawings, paintings can also be seen on the exterior walls of village huts in certain parts of the country. The north and east of Zambia boasts some impressive rock art, which depicts daily scenes from the lives of Stone Age people.

Music and Dance

Music and dance play a pivotal role in Zambian social and religious life. From the opening of parliament to independence celebrations, no national event is complete without traditional music and dancing, some of which is dazzling.

More spectacular dances include magnificently masked dancers who perform daring feats such as dancing on a rope stretched between two tall poles. The National Dance Troupe is fabled for its energetic performances at national ceremonies.

The most celebrated of all Zambian instruments is the drum. Other Zambian instruments include horns, flutes, trumpets and the xylophone or *malimba*. The xylophone is a favourite among some traditional rulers.

When it comes to modern music Zambia is yet to come up with its own distinctive style. In the late 70s and 80s attempts were made to promote *kalindula*, a fusion of Congolese rumba rhythms and softer Zambian sounds with roots in the northern Luapula Province.

Nevertheless, a recent surge of local record companies means younger musicians are experimenting with a whole range of new sounds and that unique Zambian sound could be just around the corner.

Look out for musicians such as Glorias

Band, JK, Shatel, Nasty D, St Michael Zulu, Marsha Moyo, Jane Osbourne, Maureen Lilanda and No Parking Band.

Food and Drink

The national dish, eaten every day by millions of Zambians, is nshima and relish. Nshima is a stiff meal porridge, usually made of maize and occasionally made of sorghum or cassava meal, similar to Italy's polenta. The accompanying relish can be a stew of meat, chicken or fish or one of the numerous kinds of vegetables readily grown in the country. Outdoor cooking is part of the Zambian way of life and barbecues are very popular. Meals at most hotels, lodges, camps and restaurants are mostly European.

Seasonal fruits are abundant and include pawpaws, mangoes, avocados, bananas, oranges, grapefruit, tangerines, lemons, guavas, pineapples, sugar cane and watermelons. Zambia's bush boasts more than 100 varieties of wild fruits.

A variety of local and imported alcoholic drinks are available, including the local and popular lager Mosi, South African wine and spirits. Home-brewed beer, from the sweet munkoyo to the more potent brews, is widely drunk throughout the country.

Soft drinks include the usual global fizzy drinks, a selection of local fruit juices and mineral water. Good locally-produced tea and coffee are also available.

Language

Being a former British colony, the official language is English, which is widely spoken in towns and cities.

Even in rural areas it is usually possible to find someone who speaks some English.

Zambian English is sometimes unusual. For example, if you ask 'what time will the bus leave?' the reply may be 'Now now,' meaning soon. Or someone leaving the room may say 'I am coming,' meaning they will be returning.

Seven local languages have been

English	Nyanja	Bemba
Hello	Bwanji	Shani
Goodbye	Salani bwino	Bwino shalenipo
How are you?	Muli bwanji?	Muli shani?
I am fine	Ndili bwino	Ndifye bwino
Thank you very much	Dzikomo kwambili	Natotela sana
Good morning	Mwauka bwanji	Mwashibukeni
Good night	Gonani bwino	Sendamenipo mukwai
Where do you come from?	Muchokela kuti?	Mufuma kwi?
I come from	Ndi choka	Nafuma ku .....
What is your name?	Dzina lanu ndani?	Niwe ani shina?
My name is	Dzina langa ndi ...	Ishina lyandi nine ...

Linguistic Heritage

PETER JONES ©

Legend

#		#	
1	Lunda-Luvale	8	Lala-Lamba-Bemba
2	Lozi	9	Mambwe-Inamawanga
3	Pre-Kololo	10	Tumbuka
4	Nkoya	11	Chewa-Nyanja
5	Totela-Simaa	12	Goba
6	Tonga-Ila	13	Swahili
7	Kaonde		

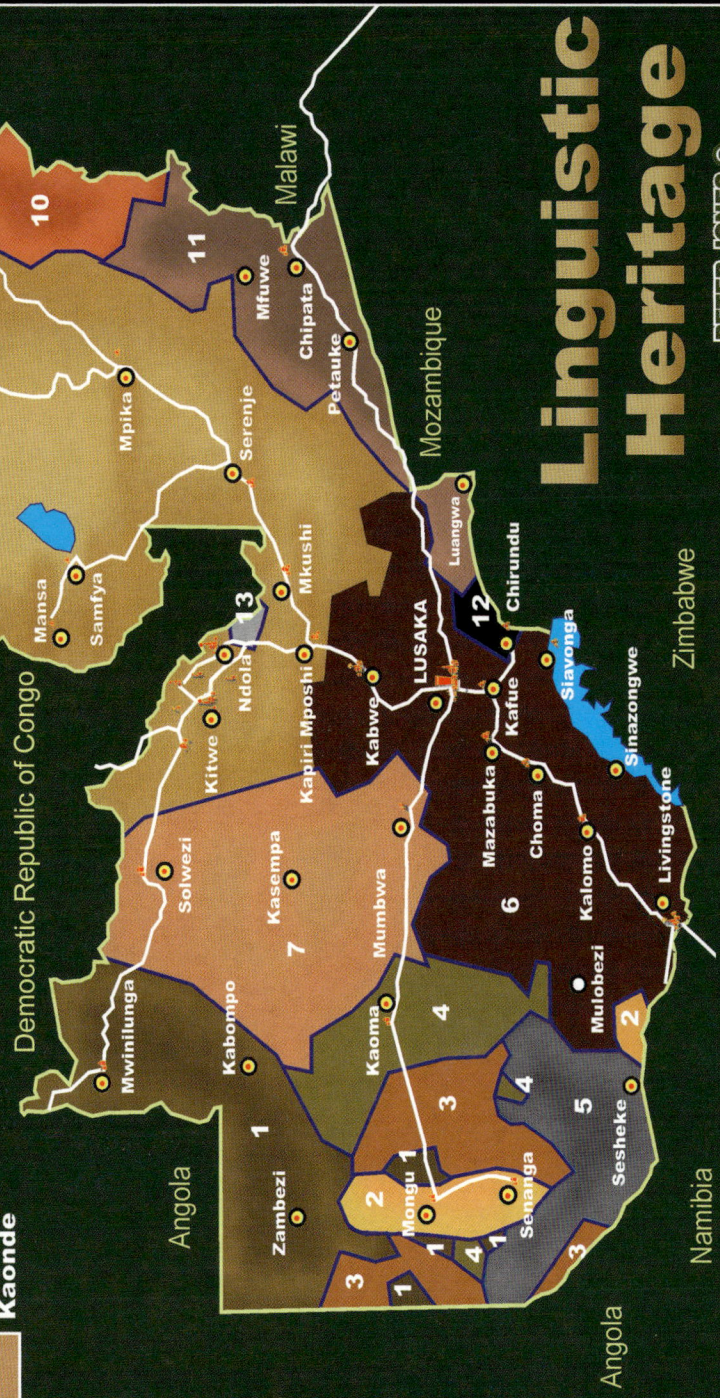

Countries

Tanzania
Malawi
Mozambique
Zimbabwe
Democratic Republic of Congo
Angola
Namibia

Places

Mbala
Mpulungu
Isoka
Mpika
Mansa
Samfya
Serenje
Mkushi
Mfuwe
Chipata
Petauke
Luangwa
Chirundu
Siavonga
Sinazongwe
Ndola
Kitwe
Kapiri Mposhi
Kabwe
LUSAKA
Kafue
Kalomo
Choma
Mazabuka
Mumbwa
Kasempa
Solwezi
Mwinilunga
Kabompo
Zambezi
Mongu
Senanga
Sesheke
Kaoma
Mulobezi
Livingstone

given special status by the government. Bemba, Kikaonde, Lozi, Lunda, Luvale, Nyanja and Tonga are used on radio, television and at primary school level. Many Zambians are able to speak more than one of these languages. Speaking a few words in the local languages is much appreciated. As Bemba and Nyanja are most widely used languages, a few useful phrases are listed on page 60.

Communications

There are post offices in all main towns and *poste restante* facilities are available. Zambia's postal services are generally safe and relatively efficient but valuable and urgent items should be sent by registered mail or via private couriers and express operators that deliver door-to-door.

Courier/postal services

DHL International Ltd Tel: 01 229768-71 Fax: 01 225529, Lusaka, *Email: dhl@lun-co.zm.dhl.com;* **Fedex** Tel: 01 252189/ 252191, Fax: 01 252585, Lusaka, *Email: keten@fedex.myexpress.co.za, Website: www.fedex.com;* **Online Express** Tel: 01 226496-7, Fax: 01 226497, Lusaka. *Email: online@zamtel.zm;* **Mercury/UPS** Tel: 01 231137/239872, Fax: 01 239868, Lusaka *Email: ups@zamnet.zm;* **Skynet Worldwide Express,** Tel: 01 224047; Fax: 01 224047, Lusaka, *Email: parexpress@zamtel.zm;* **Zampost** Tel: 01 224598/ 221707, Cairo Rd, Lusaka

Phone Services

*L*andlines are operated by the state-owned Zambia Telecommunications (Zamtel). Direct-dial international calling and fax facilities are available from post offices and telephone bureaux. Phone cards are also available from post offices, supermarkets and fuel stations. There are three cellular networks, Telecel, Celtel and Cell Z which offer pre and post paid GSM services.

Coverage is available in major towns, the network is often congested and charges are high by international standards. Visitors can buy SIM cards and rent phones, roaming is also possible.

Internet

*I*nternet services are provided by Zamtel, Zamnet, CopperNet, Uunet and Microlink Solutions. A growing number of hotels offer in-house e-mail facilities and the three major hotels in Lusaka have direct internet connections from the rooms. The larger cities have

Internet cafes:-

Businet, Tel: 01 236436; Lusaka. *Email: admin@businet.co.zm;* **LA.COM,** Tel (01) 254703. Longacres shopping centre, *Email;- ambro@zamnet.zm;* **Postnet,** Tel: 01 250966, Fax: 01 255543, Manda Hill Shopping Centre, Lusaka. *Email: postnet@zamnet.zm;* **Sternet Internet Café,** Tel: 01 220974 /229342; Fax: 01 231984, Lusaka, *Email: sternet@zamnet.zm*

The Press and Literature

*T*here are three daily newspapers: state-owned *The Daily Mail* and *Times of Zambia* and private *The Post*, all of which also publish on the weekends. The independent *Monitor* is out on Tuesdays and Fridays and *The National Mirror* once a week. The monthly *Lowdown* magazine is always worth buying for its interesting articles and listings of social events while *Trendsetters* is interesting for younger readers. A selection of imported English language newspapers and magazines are also available.

Zambia has a strong and original oral tradition of folktales, legends, proverbs and poetry, which, with its own rules of style, characterization, plot and dialogue, is sometimes incomprehensible to the western reader. Nevertheless, it still outshines the limited choice of written literature.

Try *Traditional African Tales - Stories from Zambia*, a collection of folk stories retold by local Brian Zanji. Most local writing is in English and usually concerned with religious, political or social issues.

Broadcasting

Television is dominated by government-controlled Zambia National Broadcasting Corporation, which transmits an eclectic mixture of news in English and local languages, current affairs, football games, religious programmes, documentaries, imported soaps and old films. Religious programmes are transmitted by the American Christian Television station and Trinity Broadcasting Network (TBN) while satellite TV is available via DSTV and M-Net, a South African pay -TV service. There are a number of video rental shops, including Blockbusters at Arcades, Kabulonga and Castle.

ZNBC broadcasts by radio throughout the day on many wavelengths in English and the seven major languages. Local radio stations have blossomed in recent years: Radio Christian Voice and Radio Icengelo broadcast Christian programmes, commercial stations Radio Phoenix, Choice FM and QFM transmit local news and information, sport, music and a range of features programmes. BBC World Service is available on 98 FM.

Tipping

Hotels and restaurants add a 10 per cent service charge and 17.5 per cent VAT to bills, so it is not necessary to tip but feel free to if you want. Often quoted prices do not include these extras so be careful.

Time

Zambia is two hours ahead of Greenwich Mean Time and locally people use the 24-hour clock.

Climate

There are three main seasons: the cold, dry winter season (May - August) the hot, dry season (September-November); and the warm, rainy season (December - April). Rainfall varies countrywide from 600mm to 3000mm.

Zambia's altitude means it is seldom unpleasantly hot and humidity is low. In winter the days are generally dry and sunny with temperatures averaging 15 - 20°C. But at night it can get very chilly, especially in the bush. In the hot season temperatures average 25 - 30°c during the day, except in October when temperatures often exceed 32°C.

Clothing

Bring light clothing, such as cotton, for the hot season, a light raincoat and umbrella for the rainy season, warm jumpers and fleeces for the cooler months. Even in the hotter months something warm may be needed in the mornings and evenings. Sunblock, sunglasses and hats are recommended all year round, as is a good pair of walking shoes. For game viewing you'll need dark or neutral coloured clothes. Some hotels expect smart casual wear for dining, but for the most part dress is informal though never sloppy.

Entry Requirements

All visitors require valid passports. Visas are required by most nationals but check with local Zambian embassies. Tourists entering the country as part of a tour organized by Zambian travel operators are exempt from visa requirements. Visa requirements change from time to time so be sure to check before travelling.

Border posts

Zambia can be entered by road from Botswana, Democratic Republic of Congo, Malawi, Mozambique, Namibia, Tanzania and Zimbabwe. The Angolan border is not open to road traffic due to decades of conflict. Most border posts are open from 06:00- 18:00 hours daily. Check with local residents and travel agents.

Personal Security

Zambia is generally quite a safe country and the vast majority of Zambians welcome tourists and want to be helpful, but the following precautions should be taken. Always take good care of personal valuables as pickpockets and other thieves do operate in the big cities. Crowded areas are particularly high risk. When you don't need them it is wise to keep valuables in hotel safes.

It is illegal to use, possess or trade in any kind of narcotic, and the courts are particularly severe on anyone involved with drugs. It is also illegal to import firearms into Zambia without special permission. There are also tough laws against pornography. If you are robbed, contact the police as soon as possible. Be polite in your official dealings with the police. They may request a favour in return for doing their job. If you need a copy of a crime report for insurance purposes please ensure you explain this to the police officers. As well as main police stations there are community police posts in residential, commercial and industrial areas. It is important to carry your passport at all times or at least a photocopy. Always keep a separate note of the number and its date and place of issue. If you have this information it will be easier to replace. In case you do lose your passport or it is stolen, inform the police and your embassy immediately. If you have a genuine emergency, your embassy or consulate should provide help.

Disabled Access

Facilities for the disabled are limited in Zambia and it is best to make your requirements known far in advance. Many hotels and guesthouses are single storey and small enough to cater for specific needs. Wheelchair users should be warned that because access ramps are rare you should be prepared to be carried; there is no shortage of willing helpers.

Electrical Supply

The electrical supply is the 220/240 volts systems and the three-pin plugs used are of the British square bayonet pin type.

Photography

Zambia is an immensely photogenic country and if you are a keen photographer, carry spare camera batteries and ample stocks of your preferred choice of film. Normal film and batteries can be found in the cities. Processing of prints is available, but not slides. Make sure you bring a dust-proof bag to keep your camera in and keep film in a cool box, especially when visiting in the hot season. For good wildlife photography a very powerful telescopic lens is essential. Be sensitive when photographing people. Most people, especially children, enjoy being photographed, but some are more reticent. Be polite and always ask before taking anyone's photograph. A polaroid camera overcomes the problem of promised photographs never sent. Some people may ask for payment and, faced by the poverty in which most Zambians live, you may be happy to oblige. Remember, however, that by indiscriminately handing out money you may be encouraging people to hassle tourists to photograph them for a price. Officially there are no longer any restrictions on what you may photograph, except military installations. However it is wise to ask first.

PUBLIC HOLIDAYS

1 January –	New Year's Day
12 March –	Youth Day
March/April –	Good Friday
March/April –	Holy Saturday
1 May –	Labour Day
25 May –	Africa Freedom Day
1st Monday in July –	Heroes Day
!st Tuesday in July –	Unity Day
1st Monday in August –	Farmers' Day
24 October –	Independence Day
25 December –	Christmas Day

Air Travel

Zambia is a large country and travelling by air, though expensive, can save valuable time for visitors on a short trip. Zambian Airways operate internal flights to Ndola, Kitwe, Livingstone and Mfuwe (for South Luangwa). The advent of companies such as Nationwide and British Airways mean there are often some real bargain flights between Zambia and Johannesburg and Cape Town. South African Airways also operates the South African route. Other foreign airlines are Air Malawi, Air Namibia, Air Tanzania, Air Zimbabwe, British Airways, Ethiopian Airlines, Kenya Airways and KLM.

There are also a number of charter companies, some of which operate a service on more popular routes, such as Lusaka-Mfuwe and Lusaka-Livingstone. A large group can always charter their own plane in order to reach more remote areas. All visitors are required to pay international airport tax (US$20 in US dollars) when leaving and a domestic departure fee (US$5) for internal flights. Prices are subject to change.

Air Charter

Avocet Tel: 01 236437; Fax: 01 229261
Email: avocet@zamnet.zm, Lusaka

TIAC Tel: 02 311369/311212
Chingola, Copperbelt

Experience Zambia with us.

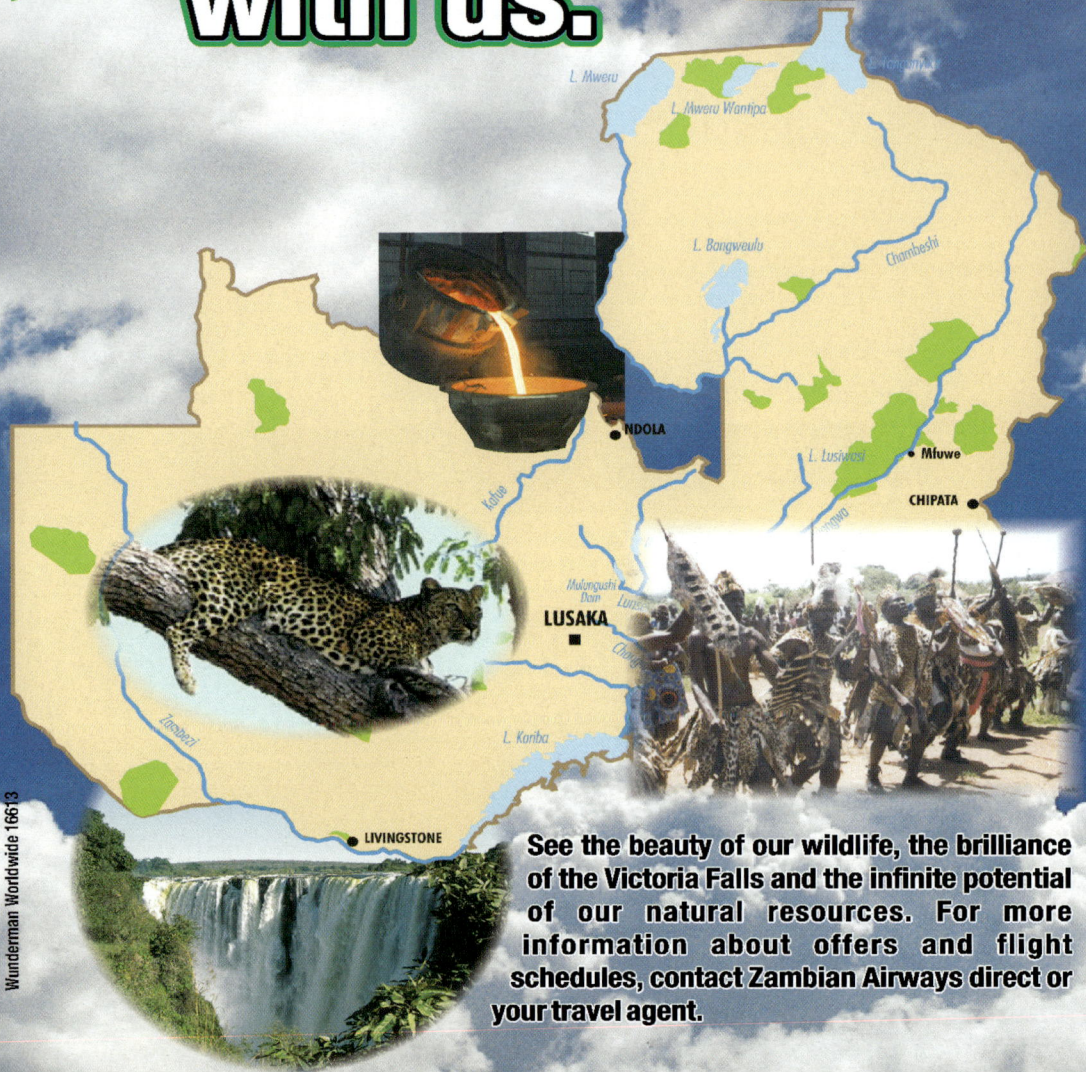

See the beauty of our wildlife, the brilliance of the Victoria Falls and the infinite potential of our natural resources. For more information about offers and flight schedules, contact Zambian Airways direct or your travel agent.

Wunderman Worldwide 16613

ZAMBIANAirways
CHANGING THE WAY AFRICA FLIES

Stabo Air Tel: 01 235976
Fax: 01 233481, Lusaka
Email: stabo@zamnet.zm

Staravia Air Charter Tel: 01 271332
(096) 750800; Fax: 01 291962, Lusaka
Email: staravia@zamnet.zm

Travel International Air Charter
Tel: 02 313521; Cel: 096780268
Email: tiac@zamtel.zm,Chingola

Airlines

Air Malawi Tel: 01 228120/1/3;
Fax: 01 228124, Lusaka
Email: airmalawi@zamnet.zm

Air Tanzania Tel: 01 251189/252499
Fax: 01 252399, Lusaka

Air Zimbabwe   Tel: 01 221750 /225431;
Fax: 01 225540, Lusaka
Email: airzim@zamtel.zm

Airwaves Avocet Tel: 01 224334/223952
Fax: 01 224334 , Lusaka
Email: airwaves@zamnet.zm

British Airways Tel: 01 255320/250579
Fax: 01 250623, Lusaka
Email:
contact.1.zambia@britishairways.com
Website: www.britishairways.com

Emirate Airlines Tel: 01 226568
Fax: 01 234491
Email: emirates@zamnet.zm

Interair Tel: 02 618083/618087/620541
Fax: 02 620542, Ndola
Tel: 01 232934, Lusaka

Kenya Airways Tel: 01 228886
Fax: 01 228902, Lusaka
Email: kqsales@zamnet.zm

KLM Royal Dutch Airlines
Tel: 01 228886; Fax: 01 228902, Lusaka
Email: klm@zamnet.zm
Email: kqsales@zamnet.zm

Nationwide Airlines - Lusaka
Tel: 01 250746, Arcades Shopping Mall

Nationwide Airlines - Livingstone
Tel: 03 323360 / 323809; Fax: 03 320609,
Email: nationwide@zamnet.zm
Website: www.flynationwide.co.za

Ndola National Airport Tel: 02 611193
/611194; Fax: 02 612635, Ndola

South African Airways Tel: 01 254350
Fax: 01 254065, Lusaka
Email: saa@zamnet.zm

Zambian Airways Tel: 01 256586/88
/225151; Fax: 01 256589, Lusaka
roanhq@zamnet.zm

"Serving Zambia's Tourism

for over 10 years"

Scheduled Services and Charter:-

	FROM	TO	ETD	ETA	COMMENTS
SUN	LUN	MFU	09:00	10:30	Off BA overnight
	LUN	MFU	14:00	15:30	Off SA & BA Comair
MON	MFU	JEK	10:00	11:20	Onto LVI SA & BA Comair
	JEK	LUN	11:30	12:00	
	LUN	LVI	12:45	14:15	
TUE	LVI	LUN	11:30	13:00	Onto **MFU JEK** SA BA Comair
	LUN	JEKI	13:45	14:15	
	JEKI	MFU	14:30	15:50	
WED	MFU	JEK	10:00	11:20	
	JEK	LUN	11:30	12:00	
	LUN	LVI	12:45	14:15	
	MFU	LUN	17:00	18:30	
THU	LVI	LUN	11:30	13:00	Off **MFU JEK SA BA Comair**
	LUN	JEKI	13:45	14:15	
	JEKI	MFU	14:30	15:50	
FRI	MFU	JEK	10:00	11:20	Onto LVI SA BA Comair
	JEK	LUN	11:30	12:00	
	LUN	LVI	12:45	14:15	
SAT	LVI	LUN	11:30	13:00	Off MFU JEK SA BA Comair
	LUN	JEKI	13:45	14:15	
	JEKI	MFU	14:300	15:50	
	MFU	LUN	17:00	18:30	**Onto BA London**

FARES	5797	FROM	TO	US$		FROM	TO	US$
		LUN	MFU	160.00		LVI	MFU	285.00
		LUN	JEKI	75.00		MFU	JEKI	200.00
		LUN	LVI	140.00				

PROFLIGHT AIR SERVICES LIMITED

P.O. Box 30536, Lusaka, Zambia, Tel: +260-1-263686/7, 233422, 233388
Cell: 096-764623, Fax: +260-1-261941/263687
Airport Office: Tel: +260-1-271139/271035
e-mail: proflite@zamnet.zm   website: www.zambiz.co.zm/proflite

SOUTH END, CAIRO ROAD

Bus Services

Most towns have a main bus station, usually close to a market. The cities have several including one or two for long distance routes.

Minibuses. These light blue and white vehicles are not for the faint-hearted nor long journeys. They are a cheap way of getting around towns, but they are overcrowded and uncomfortable. Buses leave starting points when they are full, with conductors shouting out the destination of their buses.

Always double-check the destination before boarding and confirm the prices with other passengers. You pay the conductor either as you get on or during the journey. Have as close to the exact amount as possible and be prepared to ask for your change several times. Be warned that most bus drivers might drive quickly.

Minibuses are a favourite target at police roadblocks so be prepared for delays.

Buses. For longer distances, including travelling to other countries, there are a number of companies offering travel by ordinary bus, express coaches and luxury express coaches. Travel is relatively cheap and it is worth paying the little bit extra to get the extra comfort of luxury coaches.

On all three types of buses, overcrowding is virtually unheard of, there is a flexible timetable and many have their own station.

The fare is paid in advance. If there is no timetable, ask around to discover a plausible departure time or simply arrive early at the bus station. Bear in mind that more buses leave in the morning so as to cover long distances during daylight. Some drivers are very fast and dangerous.

CR Coaches located at Intercity Bus terminal, Lusaka; Intercape Mainliner, Tel: 01 251358, Email: info@intercape.co.za, Lusaka; Linking Africa Tel: 01 234420, Lusaka; Trans Zambezi, Tel: 01 251369/ 22, Fax: 01 254917, Lusaka, Email: info@intercape .co.za, Website: www.intercape.co.za; Translux Bus Services, Tel: 01 228682/ 228683 Email: reservations@zamsaf.co.zm,Lusaka

Car Hire

Renting a car is an expensive option but a convenient way of seeing more of the off-the-beaten-track sights. There are local and international car rental companies in Lusaka, Livingstone, Kitwe and Ndola.

AVIS RENT A CAR
Avis Rent A Car

Avis Rent a Car
Tel: 01 271303; Fax: 01 252201, Lusaka.
Email: avis@zamnet.zm

Tel: 02 620741 /097 800756, Ndola

Taiwo Car Hire
Tel: (097) 789268/ 01
291283/294015; Fax: 01
291248, Lusaka.
Email: taiwo@zamnet.zm
Website: www.taiwo.co.za

Chita Car Hire
Tel: 01 255789/255790
Fax: 01 255789, Lusaka
Email: chitacar@zamnet.zm

Imperial Car Rental
Tel: 02 311642 /311722;
Fax:02 312552, Chingola
Email: voychin@zamnet.zm

Tel: 02 225056 /227169;
Fax:02 224834, **Kitwe**
Email: voykitwe@coppernet.zm

Tel: (03) 322753
Fax:(03) 320277, **Livingstone**
Email: imperial@zamnet.zm

Tel: 02 620604 /617062;
Fax:02 620605, **Ndola**
Email: voyrent@coppernet.zm

AVIS RENT A CAR
Avis Rent A Car

ZAMBIA

38645 Lusaka, Zambia
Holiday Inn, Church Road
Lusaka, Zambia

☎ (2601) 251642/251652
FAX (2601) 252201

Lusaka Airport
☎ (2601) 271090
24 hrs Emergency
Cell : 097 773978
E-mail : avis@zamnet.zm

Ndola Airport
☎ (2602) 620741
Cell : 097 800756

Livingstone Airport
Cell : 097 780670

AVIS

We try harder.

73

Livingstone 4x4 Hire Tel: 03 320888/7
Fax: 03 320887, Livingstone
Email: 4x4hire@zamnet.zm
Website: www.4x4hireafrica.com

Monomatapa Car Hire Tel: 03 322729
/097 806459, Livingstone
Email: solankis@zamnet.zm

Sepiso Car Rentals Tel: 01 220388 /097
846742; Fax: 01 225462, Lusaka
Email: sepiso@zamnet.zm
Website: www.sepisocarhire.com

Trains

Train travel in Zambia is slow and uncomfortable. Railway Systems of Zambia operates the Lusaka-Ndola-Kitwe and Lusaka-Livingstone routes while Tanzania-Zambia Railways (Tazara) runs between Kapiri-Mposhi and the Tanzanian capital Dar-es-Salaam.

Standards on Tazara service have been improved in recent years although they are still not brilliant. Neverthless, if you bring plenty of water, the three-day journey through beautiful national parks and in the company of eclectic passengers is quite an experience. It is worth the extra cost to travel in first-class, which is still basic. Booking is essential.

Tazara Email: acistz@twiga.com;
Railway Systems of Zambia,
Tel: 01 228023 /222562, Lusaka

Taxis

Private taxis are unmetered so negotiate the fare before you get in. Most drivers will try to make a quick buck out of visitors so do not be afraid to bargain, though do this politely and with a smile. Most hotels will be able to advise what you should be charged. Ensure you have the change or ask the driver if he has some, otherwise you may end up paying more than agreed.
Dial-A-Cab Tel: 095 701377/096 222222/097 773937
Lusaka

Motoring

If you are bringing a motor vehicle into the country you must have a Customs Importation Permit (CIP), which is issued at your border point of entry. You must carry the CIP, the vehicle's insurance papers and valid international or SADC driving licence in the car at all times as the police are entitled to ask for these documents at the countless roadblocks set up on Zambia's major roads. You should be aware that these checkpoints are ostensibly set up for security purposes. Remember to carry all the right documents, wear your seatbelt, carry warning triangles, red and white reflective strips on the vehicle is a legal requirement in Zambia. Adherence to the above should make your journey hassle-free.

Driving is on the left, the speed limit is 50km per hour in built up areas and 120km per hour on the open road with 100km per hour when leaving builtup areas. Be careful of speed traps.

In urban areas watch out for cyclists, while in rural areas domestic and wild animals on or near the road can also be extremely hazardous. Road signage is basic and street names and building numbers often non-existent.

There are petrol stations in main towns, where fuel is paid for in cash. Sometimes, especially in smaller towns, there is no fuel so ensure that you have a full tank before setting off and fill up whenever you can. Always carry jerry cans of fuel and water for long distance journeys rather than resort to buying from the roadside (marked by plastic containers and bottles) as more often than not this fuel is contaminated. To avoid potholes, vehicles often keep on the best part of the road until they have to pass each other. It is also accepted practice to honk your horn to warn pedestrians and other motorists as you approach.

Start off early and plan ahead to avoid driving at night, a highly dangerous undertaking given the number of potholes and vehicles with one or no lights on the road. Equally dangerous, at night and during the day, is a vehicle broken down on the road. Be aware that most vehicles do not carry red warning triangles so the first signs of a breakdown are often a hard-to-see trail of branches and foliage on the road. Make sure you carry all breakdown equipment, including an inflated spare tyre, a jack in working order, the correct size wheel spanner and a puncture repair kit. Spare tools are hard to find beyond major cities. There is no metered parking, but you may have to pay a small fee to local council workers for certain parking spaces in town.

More often young men will offer to watch your vehicle for a small fee. Never park in an unguarded area and do not leave anything of value visible in your car.

Car Services

Cycling

Cycling tourists are still rare in Zambia, except in the Livingstone area where bicycles can be hired.

As yet no one offers cycling tours, so if you want to brave long distances and bad roads then you will have to make your own arrangements. Get plenty of advice before starting out.

HitchHiking

Hitch hiking is common where public transport is scarce.

Locals almost always pay for the ride and you will be expected to do the same.

Travel & Tour Operators

Terrain tamer Totally tough Totally Toyota
Toyota Hilux 3000DE.
The vehicle that's united nations.

From Zambia to Zanzibar, the Hilux has been trusted throughout Africa for over 40 years. Now, with its improved 3000 DE engine, the new Hilux maintains that tradition of never-say-die toughness and reliability. So whatever NGO or company you're with, you can rely on your Hilux to accomplish your mission.

We provide Quality cars for Hire:

- Volkswagen : Jetta, Golf & Polo
- Toyota   : Hilux 4 x 4, Camry, Corona,
                Corolla, Isuzu 4x2, Nissan Hard Body 4 x4

Cars are available Chauffeur Driven or Self Drive,

VOLARE TOURS & TRAVEL LTD

卐   Domestic Ticketing
卐   International Ticketing
卐   Board Meetings, Conferences
卐   First Hand information on Lodges in Zambia enabling us to
       tailor your tips to your preferences.

IATA
MEMBER OF IATA

RESERVATION
NDOLA OFFICE
H 9 Arusha Street,
P.O. Box 70199
Tel: 618861 / 618862
Fax: 613941 / 618861

CELL NOS:
096-901793
096-905259
096-781068
097-829223

RESERVATION
CHINGOLA
Standard Chartered Bank Building
1st Floor
Plot 142 - 51 Kwacha St. Chingola
Tel: 312651 / 311620 Fax: 311620

WILD SIDE
TOURS AND SAFARIS

Wildside Tours & Safaris
Tel: 03 323726;Cel +263 11 211103
Fax: 03 322895, Livingstone,
Email: wild@zamnet.zm
Website: www.wildsidesafaris.com

Royal Travel and Tours,
Tel: 02 612412 429;
Fax:02 617518, Ndola
Email: royal@coppernet.zm

Kachelo Travel Ltd
Tel: 01 263973 /260817
/(097) 807083;
Fax: 265560, Lusaka
Email: kachelo@zamnet.zm

Wild Tracks

Wild Tracks Tel: 01 251071
Fax: 01 250890, Lusaka
Email: wild@zamnet.zm
Website: www.wildtracks.info

Juls Limited
Travel, Car Hire, Tours & Guest House

The real Africa - an experience you'll never forget

Travel

Juls Travel team is well trained in travel
management and can take you anywhere
in the world, with ease. All it takes is a
Telephone call and your travel needs are
met by our experienced team.

Tours

Our Tour operators offer tailor made tours to any
destination in Zambia and the rest of the region.
Just email or fax your itinerary and we will do the
rest.

Car Hire

Juls Car Hire is the ultimate in road transport,
with its wide range of air-conditioned vehicles,
consisting of minibuses, four wheel drive and
saloon cars.

Guest House

While you are enjoying the best of Africa's wild
life, why not break your journey and spend a few
nights at Juls Guest House and sample some of
the many excellent restaurants around or simply
relax and enjoy Juls own home made meals .

CONTACT DETAILS ARE:
Tel: 260-1-292979 / 293972
Fax: 260-1-291246
Postal address: Postnet No. 79, Pvt. Bag E891,
Lusaka, Zambia
e-mail: julscar@zamnet.zm
Website: www.zambiatourism.com/juls
www.julstravel.com

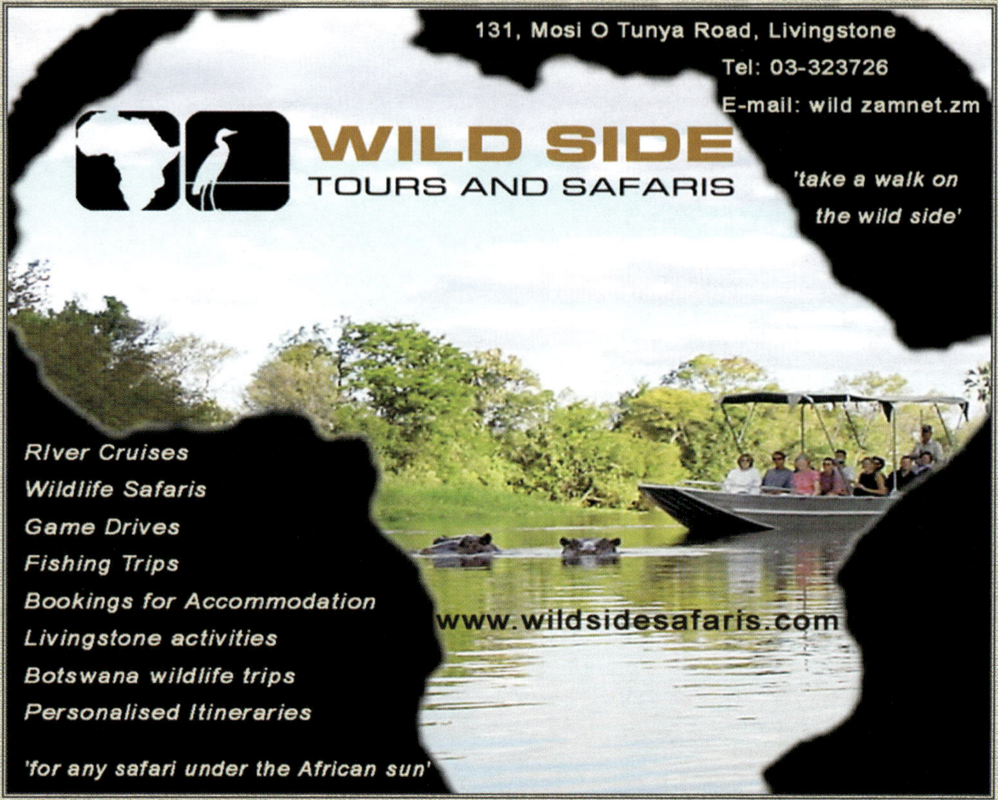

Addit Travel and Tours
Tel: 01 228792/ 4, 220469; Fax: 01
222655, Lusaka
Email: astro@zamnet.zm

Livingstone Safaris
Tel: (03) 322267
Livingstone
Email: geckos@zamnet.zm

Airmasters Travel & Tours
Tel: 01 236984, 221708
Fax: 01 220898, Lusaka
Email: airmast@zantel.zm

Premier Travel & Tours
Tel: 01 222931 /224138 /226121;
Fax: 01 222710, Lusaka
Email: premier@zamtel.zm

Tel: 02 230123 /4;
Fax:02 230121, Kitwe
Email: att@coppernet.zm

Professional Travel & Tours
Tel: 01 225433;
Fax: 01 224815, Lusaka

Fairland Tours & Travel Services Ltd
Tel: 01 225822, 097 806355/843201
Fax: 01 223976, Lusaka
Email: catherinemunba@yahoo.com

Tel: 02 610273-6;
Fax:02 615245, Ndola
Email: protrav@zamnet.zm

Sky Jet Travel Limited
Tel: 01 255607/8
Fax: 01 255089, Lusaka
Email: skyjet@zamnet.zm

Shiwa Safaris Tel: 01 228682 /3;
Fax: 01 222906, Lusaka
Email: reservations@zamsaf.com

Steve Blagus
Tel: 01 227739/40
Fax:01 225178, **Lusaka**
Email: sblagus@zamnet.zm

Tel: 02 610993/610994
Fax:02 619072, **Ndola**
Email: blagusnl@zamnet.zm

Tara Travel & Tours Ltd Tel: 01 252174
/252371, 096 759059/953023;
Fax: 01 252371, Lusaka
Email: tarratt@zamnet.zm

Top Flight Travel & Tours
Tel: 01 224417 /224436/ 18;
Fax: 01 224445, Lusaka
Email: topflight@zamnet.zm

Trek Africa Tel: 02 224350/224277
Fax:02 227217, Kitwe
Email: kitwe@trekafrica.com.zm

United Tour Company
Telfaxl: 03 323095, Livingstone
Email: utc@zamnet.zm

Voyagers Travel & Tours
Tel: 01 253082/3/4
Fax: 01 253048, **Lusaka**
Email: voytrav@zamnet.zm
Website: www.voyagerzambia.com

Tel: 02 311722, 312195
Fax:02 312552, **Chingola**
Email: voychin@zamnet.zm

Tel: 02 229102/3;
Fax:02 224834, **Kitwe**
Email: voykitwe@coppernet.zm

Tel: 02 621335/6;
Fax:02 621331, **Ndola**
Email: voyagers@zamnet.zm

Zambian Safari Company Tel: 01 228682
/3; Fax: 01 222609, Lusaka
Email: reservations@zamsaf.com

Zata Travel & Tours Tel: 01 236764
/236838; Fax:01 236765, Lusaka

International Tour Operators
Acacia Expeditions
Overland tours/camping trips for travelers on low and medium budgets in Zambia/ Southern Africa
23a Craven Terrace,
Lancaster Gate, London W2 3QH
www.acacia-africa.com

Classics Camps of Africa Association of independent camps including Tena Tena, Sausage Tree and Tongabezi in Zambia
Tel: + 27 11 463 8622
Fax: + 27 11 463 8196
classics@classicsafaricamps.com
www.classicsafaricamps.com

Explore Worldwide
Tours for small groups in the Luangwa valley. 1 Fredrick st, Aldershot,
Hampshire GU 1LQ
Email: info@exploreworldwide.com

Sunvil Discovery
This is UK's leading Zambia specialist offering a wide range of good value safaris
Sunvil House, Upper Square
Old Isleworth TW7 7 BJ
Email: africa@sunvil.co.uk

Zambia Outdoor
Specialises in tour safaris all over Zambia
Email: info@zambiaoutdoor.com.uk

Changing Money

The unit of currency is the Kwacha (K). Banknotes come in denominations of K50,000, K10 000, K5 000, K1 000, K500, K100, K50 and K20. Coins are no longer used. There is no restriction on the amount of foreign currency notes visitors may bring into Zambia. In general, cash in US dollars or British pounds are most convenient and fetch the best rates. Travellers cheques are the safest since they can be replaced if lost or stolen. Major banks, including Barclays, Standard Chartered and Stanbic will accept them, but the rate will be lower and you willl be charged commission.

Major credit cards such as Visa, American Express, Master card and Diners' Club are accepted in upmarket hotels and restaurants, and to pay for flights, tours and car rentals. But many places still accept cash only. Do not be tempted to deal with money-changers on the street and at border posts. They are shrewd operators and, if you do not get cheated with the rate, you could end up with a fistful of counterfeit notes. Politely say no and shop around increasingly competitive banks and bureaux de change.

Always be careful with your money and credit cards. Given Zambian prices, it is sometimes hard to avoid carrying large sums of cash with you, but try to carry enough only for your immediate needs.

Money Transfers

Immediate money transfers can be made, at a cost, via the Western Union.
Western Union Money Transfers
Tel: 01 234407 / 221707 / 226220
Fax: 01 234407
Email: zampost@zamnet.zm
Website: www.westernunion.com
Lusaka.

Health Precautions

Malaria is prevalent in Zambia and visitors are strongly advised to take a number of precautionary measures, including a course in prophylactic (preventive) drugs that covers the period immediately before and after your trip. Ask your doctor for the latest information on which drugs you should take.

The best way of keeping mosquitoes away at night is to spray your hotel room or light a mosquito coil and sleep under a mosquito net, preferably one impregnated with insecticide. If the windows and doors in your room are not screened with mosquito netting, keep them closed.

Always apply mosquito repellents and wear long sleeved clothing and long trousers, especially if you are outdoors in the evening.

If you do develop symptoms (high

fever, shivering, headaches), seek medical attention immediately. It is extremely important to report to the nearest health facility as soon as possible for proper diagnosis, which involves a blood test, and prompt treatment. Even if you do not test positive the first time, if your symptoms continue chances are you do have malaria and must treat it. Malaria is dangerous and can be fatal if not treated quickly.

Malaria has an incubation period that ranges from a few days to several weeks so you can become ill long after being bitten. If you get flu-like symptoms once you are back home, seek medical attention and inform your doctor that you have recently visited a malaria zone.

The HIV/AIDS pandemic has hit Zambia hard, with about 20 per cent of the population infected. You are putting yourself in great danger if you have unprotected sex. Reduce the risk by using a condom.

Blood to be used for transfusion has been tested for HIV for several years. However, it is best you know your blood group, and if possible draw up a list of potential blood donors who can be contacted if necessary. Ensure your medical kit has some syringes just in case.

To avoid an upset stomach, be careful about what you eat and drink. Stick to bottled or treated water (it's a good idea to carry water purification tablets especially if you are traveling off the beaten track) and avoid foods cooked in unhygienic circumstances or raw vegetables and salad.

Most stomach upsets will be minor and should clear up with appropriate medicine. But if the symptoms persist and you have been living rough, a blood test may be worthwhile to see whether you have picked up a more serious parasite.

Avoid sunstroke by staying out of the midday sun. Avoid swimming in rivers, lakes and dams as they may be infected with bilharzia, a disease spread by water-snails.

All clothes washed and hung in the open air to dry should be ironed to kill the eggs of the putsi fly, which lays eggs on damp clothing, and is very painful.

Before you leave home, take out suitable medical insurance (watch out for exclusion clauses!), have a dental check-up, and if you wear glasses or contact lenses carry the prescription and spare pairs. If you suffer from a chronic disease such as diabetes or high blood pressure, arrange for a check-up with your doctor who can supply an adequate supply of medication.

A letter explaining your health problems and/ or drugs you are taking may help if you find yourself having health problems. Even if your heath is good, it is advisable to pack a fully stocked medical kit. All major towns have state-run hospitals and private clinics.

Privately run hospitals are restricted to the cities.

In smaller towns and rural settlements there are hospitals run by the church and government clinics. While private medical facilities are reasonably well-stocked, state-run hospitals are poorly equipped and there are often shortages of drugs. Keep your personal medication and your contact lenses in your hand luggage when travelling in case your luggage is delayed on route.

Pharmacists are helpful, but in most cases will not dispense drugs without a doctor's prescription.

Please note that most medication is imported and certain drugs are not readily available. In emergencies, medical emergency intervention and evacuation services will fly patients to South Africa, such as **MARS International** Tel (01) 234290/2 Lusaka and Tel (02) 230715/6 Kitwe and **Speciality Emergency Services** Tel (01) 273302/7, 097 770302/3. Services are efficient and extend to the most remote regions of the country. Most forms of rescue transport have ICU facilities.

Clinics / Hospitals

Chingola
Chingola Mines Hospital
Tel (02) 349555

Zambia Consolidated Copper Mining
Tel (02) 349004,
Fax (02) 312039

Chipata
Chipata General,
Tel (062) 22304

Chipata Medical Care,
Tel (062) 22507 / 21663,
Fax (062) 21663,

Chirundu
Chirundu Hospital

Choma
Choma Hospital,
Tel (032) 20588/9

Macha Mission Hospital
Tel (032) 20778

Kabwe
Kabwe General Hospital
Tel (05) 222301,

Kabwe Mine Hospital
Tel (05) 247359 / 222564

Kalomo
Kalomo Hospital,
Tel (032) 65235

Kaoma
Kaoma Hospital, Tel (07) 360107

Kapiri Mposhi
Selah Medical Centre,
Tel (05) 271023,

Kasama
Kasama Hospital, Tel (04) 222041

Kitwe
Company Clinic,
Tel (02) 225693 / 223939 (01) 705033
Fax (02) 225772

Kitwe General, Tel (02) 228011

Nkana General Hospital
Tel (02) 227355

Nkana Mines Hospital
Tel (02) 243555

Wusakile Hospital,
Tel (02) 224144

Livingstone
Livingstone General Hospital
Tel (03) 320221

Luanshya
Luanshya Hospital, Tel (02) 511311

Roan Antelope Hospital
Tel (02) 544202 / 549020 / 549555
Fax (02) 544099

Lusaka
Care for Business Clinic
Tel 254396/9

Chainama Hills Hospital, Tel 292444

City Medical Centre, Tel 252450

Coptic Clinic, Tel 237584,
Fax 236587

Fairview Clinic, Tel 229278
Family Medical Clinic
Tel 222540 / 227304,
Fax 226891

Grand Medical Centre, Tel 223263

Hilltop Hospital, Tel 263407 / 263452
Fax 264919

Italian Orthopaedic Hospital
Tel 254601,
Fax 255113

K.G. Dental Surgery, Tel 292219

Magnum Medical Clinic
Tel 262420 / 262366,
Fax 252371

Maina Soko Hospital,
Tel 260301/3
Fax 263883

Midlands Medical Center
Tel 251123

Minbank Clinic, Tel 226983
Fax 222612

St Josephs Hospital
Tel 261247 / 260492,
Fax 251154

Mutti Clinic, Tel 227178

Primary Care Clinic
Tel 251152 / 251194

Teba Medical Centre, Tel 290141
Fax 294996

University Teaching Hospital
Tel 251430 / 251445 / 251200 / 251447
Fax 251451

Woodlands Surgery, Tel 26236
ZCCM Mine Hospital, Tel 253481
Fax 250989

Maamba
Maamba Hospital
Tel (032) 78080 / 78201 / 78141/2

Mazabuka
Chikinkata Hospital, Tel (032) 30110

Mazabuka Hospital
Tel (032) 30205 / 30188 / 30130 / 30951

Mbala
Mbala General Hospital
Tel (04) 450111

Mongu
Mongu Lewanika Hospital
Tel (07) 221011

Monze
Monze General Hospital
Tel (032) 50171

Mpika
Mpika Hospital, Tel (04) 370658

Mufulira
Mufulira Hospital
Tel (02) 411644 / 411703 / 412666

Munbwa
Mumbwa Hospital, Tel 800111

Ndola
Miramar Clinic, Tel (02) 680077/8
Fax (02) 618197

Ndola Trust Hospital
Tel (02) 614604

Solwezi
Solwezi Hospital, Tel (08) 821011/2

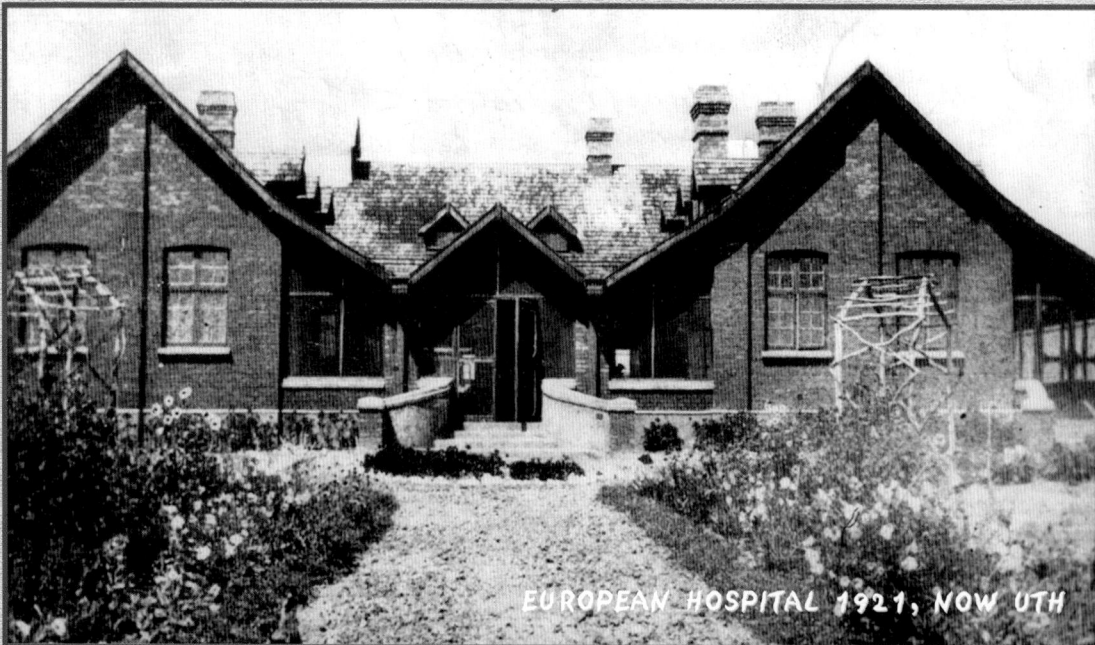

EUROPEAN HOSPITAL 1921, NOW UTH

FINDECO HOUSE, CAIRO ROAD

COSMOPOLITAN LUSAKA

Lusaka has long attracted rural Zambians and foreigners, which has created an increasingly lively and cosmopolitan feel to Zambia's capital.

The city is a peculiar mix of the modern and the old, at times the pace is unhurried and relaxed, at other times frenetic, especially if you get caught up in one of Lusaka's chaotic traffic jams. Some of the streets are lined with beautiful flowering trees such as jacaranda, flamboyant and frangipani, others choked with rubbish.

Lusaka ballooned from a quiet, provincial settlement less than a century ago into a sprawling city of about two million.

It traces its roots back to 1905 when the railway engineers building the Livingstone-Broken Hill (present-day Kabwe) railway established a railway siding near the small Lenje village of Chief Lusaakas.

Within five years Europeans settled in, building a post office, police station, mills, black smith's shop, a mission school, shops, a hotel, a rifle club and sports club. Over the next few decades Lusaka grew at a slow pace. However, events took a new twist in July 1931 when Lusaka was selected as the site of the new capital of Northern Rhodesia, basically because it was at the centre of the country, had an adequate water supply and a pleasant climate.

Independence and high copper prices saw Lusaka transformed overnight. Many of its dusty roads were paved and modern buildings were built, such as Findeco House (previous page) on Cairo Road, a 23-storey building of separated layers balanced on a narrow column now showing its age and poor design. The population skyrocketed as thousands of rural Zambians poured into the city hoping to find work.

With the downturn of copper prices in the mid-1970s, Zambia drifted into severe economic problems and Lusaka's ambitious building projects were put on hold. But this didn't stop the drift of job-seekers from the villages and the city bulged and groaned under the weight of people it didn't have the infrastructure to support. Shambolic and dirty shanty towns sprang up and the city fell into disrepair.

There have been recent fairly successful efforts to improve the city's image by repairing roads, clearing the streets of rubbish, painting buildings and rehabilitating green spaces. However, the rising number of street children, often left homeless because parents have died from AIDS-related diseases, a huge problem in Zambia, is disturbing.

It's a relatively safe city, although you'd be foolish to walk around after dark and as a visitor you may be targeted by pickpockets. But you should be fine if you're sensible and aware.

Lusaka is not the most fascinating place for visitors. But there are enough things to do within the city itself, including visiting interesting galleries and markets, and within easy reach outside, such as game parks and horse-riding centres, to make a few days enjoyable. And of course, Lusaka's a handy gateway for the rest of the country.

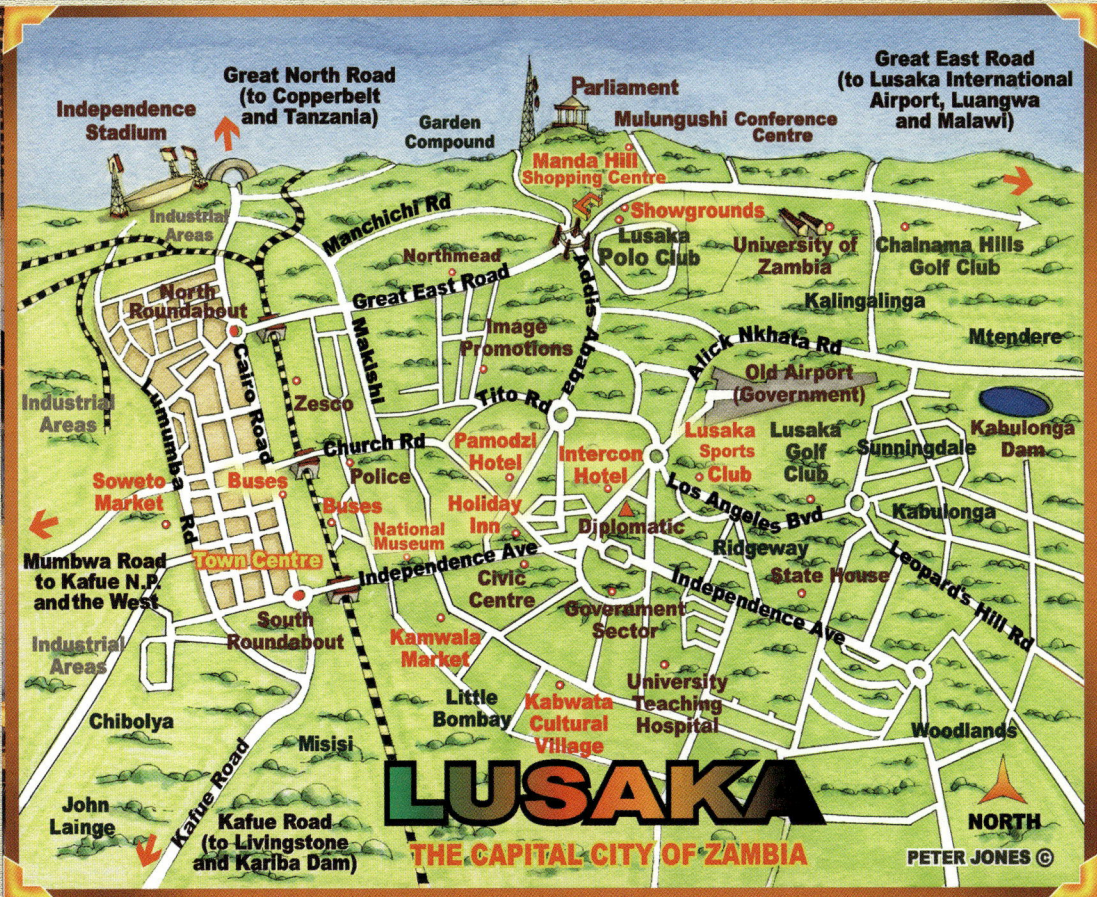

LUSAKA
THE CAPITAL CITY OF ZAMBIA

PETER JONES ©

NORTH

Great North Road (to Copperbelt and Tanzania)

Great East Road (to Lusaka International Airport, Luangwa and Malawi)

Independence Stadium

Parliament

Garden Compound

Mulungushi Conference Centre

Manda Hill Shopping Centre

Showgrounds

Industrial Areas

Manchichi Rd

Northmead

Lusaka Polo Club

University of Zambia

Chainama Hills Golf Club

North Roundabout

Great East Road

Makishi

Kalingalinga

Mtendere

Image Promotions

Alick Nkhata Rd

Industrial Areas

Limulunga Rd

Cairo Road

Zesco

Tito Rd

Old Airport (Government)

Kabulonga Dam

Church Rd

Pamodzi Hotel

Intercon Hotel

Lusaka Sports Club

Lusaka Golf Club

Sunningdale

Soweto Market

Buses

Police

Buses

Holiday Inn

Los Angeles Blvd

Kabulonga

National Museum

Diplomatic

Ridgeway

Leopard's Hill Rd

Mumbwa Road to Kafue N.P. and the West

Town Centre

Independence Ave

Civic Centre

Independence Ave

State House

South Roundabout

Kamwala Market

Government Sector

Industrial Areas

Chibolya

Misisi

Little Bombay

Kabwata Cultural Village

University Teaching Hospital

Woodlands

John Lainge

Kafue Road

Kafue Road (to Livingstone and Kariba Dam)

To the
North West

To the
Copperbelt

KAPIRI MPOSHI
812 KM
TANGANYIKA

Great North
Road

Farming
Districts

Mkushi

To
Tanzania
and the
Northeast

Kapiri Mposhi

Lukanga
Swamps

Kabwe

LUSAKA
358 KM
NDOLA

Great North
Road

Chisamba

Mulungushi
Dam

Lumsemfwa
River

Mumbwa

LUSAKA
276 KM
KAFUE NP

LUSAKA

Lusaka
International
Airport

To
Luangwa
Valley
and Malawi

To Western
Zambia

Blue Lagoon
National Park

Munda Wanga
Zoo

Zambezi River

Kafue River

Kafue

Chirundu

Lochinvar
National Park

LIVINGSTONE
472 KM
LUSAKA

Monze

Mazabuka
Farming
Districts

Siavonga

To
Zimbabwe

Choma

KARIBA

Kalomo

Home of Nyaminyami

LAKE KARIBA

To Livingstone
and
Victoria Falls

Sinazongwe

CHETE
ISLAND

CENTRAL ZAMBIA
The Capital - LUSAKA - and surrounding areas

PETER JONES ©

Wherever you stay in
the world, some things
never change.

When you stay at a Holiday Inn hotel the same first class levels of comfort, warmth and sheer hospitality apply, no matter where you are in the world. Every guest room has a telephone, radio, TV and air conditioning. There are restaurants and bars to relax in, conference and meeting facilities as well as secretarial and fax services to help you work. So, whether you're visiting Nairobi or New York you're staying at a hotel where you can be guaranteed truly international standards. It makes all the difference in the world.

Holiday Inn®

Just the way you like it

HOW TO GET THERE

By air

Lusaka International Airport, is located just outside Lusaka on the Great East Road is 26km east of the city centre.

By road

Entering Lusaka by road you will enter either from the north on Great North Road, from the east on Great East Road, from the south on Kafue or from the west on Mumbwa road.

By train

There are train services between Lusaka and Kitwe and Lusaka and Livingstone.

PLACES TO STAY

Top Range

Chrismar Hotel
Tel (01) 253036/253605
Fax (01) 252569
Los Angeles Boulevard
Email:chrismar@zamnet.zm
Web: www.chrismar.co.za. Located near the Lusaka Golf Club with a good gym.

Lilayi Lodge
Tel (01) 279023-5,
Fax (01) 279022
Lilayi Road, Off
Kafue Road, Lilayi
Email: marketing@zamsaf.co.zm
Website: www.zambiz.co.zm/lilayi/
Located just outside Lusaka, game park and lodge. Conference facilities.

Holiday Inn
Tel (01) 251666/251501
Fax (01) 253529
Corner of Church & Independence Ave.
Email: holinn@zamnet.zm
Part of the Holiday Inn Garden Court group of Hotels with attractive surroundings. It has a small residential gym, with shops, Avis Rent-A-Car, British Airways and Barclays Bank on its premises.

Hotel Inter.Continental
Tel (01) 250000/250600,Fax (01) 250895
Haile Selassie Avenue, Longacres
Email: lusaka@interconti.com
Website: www.interconti.com
Part of the Inter.Continental group of Hotels. Luxury hotel close to the diplomatic missions. Recently refurbished with gym, swimmimg pool and tennis court. Shopping mall within the hotel.

Taj Pamodzi Hotel, Tel (01) 254455, Fax (01) 254005, Church Road
Email: pamodzi@zamnet.zm
Website: www.tajhotels.com
Part of the Indian Taj group of hotels. Offers conference facilities, gym, squash court & swimming pool.

Uniquely Inter·Continental

Uniquely Lusaka

A true landmark in Zambia's capital of Lusaka, the Hotel Inter·Continental is in full operation having undergone extensive renovations in a phased manner. Ideally situated in the diplomatic area and in close proximity to the commercial centre of Lusaka, it is the ideal location for a business or leisure visit. Two hundred and twenty one newly renovated rooms, including 20 suites, are furnished and equipped to the highest Inter·Continental Hotel standards. A choice of Lusaka's leading restaurants will be found within the Hotel, including the Olive Grove where you can sample Mediterranean specialities from Italy, Spain, Greece, Morocco and Lebanon. Hotel Inter·Continental Lusaka maintains it's position as "The Meeting Place" with modern audio visual equipment and upgraded conference and banquet rooms accommodating functions of all sizes, with up to 500 people in the Ballroom. Add to this the famous friendliness of our staff and you will know what it is to enjoy a uniquely Inter·Continental stay in true Lusaka style.

HOTEL
INTER·CONTINENTAL
LUSAKA

Haile Selassie Avenue, P O Box 32201, Lusaka 10101, Zambia.
Telephone: +260 (1) 250000/250600 Facsimile: +260 (1) 251880
E-mail: lusaka@interconti.com Website: www.interconti.com

Middle Range

Lusaka Hotel, Tel (01) 229049/ 229052, Fax (01) 225726, Cairo Road, *Email: lushotel@zamnet.zm, Located in the centre of town, and* one of the oldest hotels, recently modernised.

Mulungushi Village Tel (01) 293472/ 291281, (097) 841785, Fax (01) 290830, *Email: mvc@zamnet.zm* Apartments with use of squash & tennis courts, bar, restaurant & swimming pool

GARDEN GROUP OF HOTELS

Ndeke Hotel, Tel (01) 251734/251760 Fax (01) 233264, Los Angeles Boulevard, Longacres. *Email: gardengroup@zamtel.zm Web:www.zambiatourism.com/garden-group.* Simple, safe and within walking distance of the Longacres Shopping centre.

Palm Wood Lodge and Mabels Nurseries Tel (01) 290828 Fax (01) 290828, 609 Chudleigh *Email: palmwood@zamnet.zm* Accommodation with conference & board meeting facilities

Budget

Afrikolor Guest house
Tel (01) 274686/
097 772980
Fax (01) 272694, Off Kafue Road
Email: jomurru@coppernet.zm
Off the Kafue Road set in a pretty garden.

Comfort Zone Guest House, Tel (01) 272610/ 097 891333
Fax (01) 225617,
Cassanova Rd, Makeni, Off Kafue Rd,
Email: knalf@coppernet.zm
Basic amenities

Arabian Nights, Tel (01) 295613-4/
097 779776, Fax (01) 295613
Plot 11789, Kabompo Close, Kalundu
Email: ghazi@zamnet.zm
Web: www.arabian-night.com,
Popular restaurant offering accommodation and swimming pool.

LaCabbana Lodge & Safaris
Tel (01) 293407/292813/097 784938
Fax (01) 292813, Plot 6732, Chiwala
Mabwe Rd, Olympia Ext
Email: lacabana@zamnet.zm
Basic amenities. Small business centre.

Blue Crest Guest House
Tel (01) 260536/ 096 762133
Fax (01) 267093,
15 Sable Road, Kabulonga,
Email: bluecr@coppernet.zm
Comfortable guest house with pleasant surroundings. Restaurant, bar and pool.

Johnny's Resturant & Guest House
Tel (01) 252197,
Lagos Road
Email: johnpri@hotmail.com
Comfortable rooms with basic amenities.

Juls Limited Guest House
Tel (01) 292979/293972,
Fax (01) 291246,
5507 Libala Road, Kalundu
Email: julscar@zamnet.zm
Web: www.julstravel.com, Converted villa, big, comfy rooms in pleasant surroundings. Friendly management. Car hire & travel office on premises.

GARDEN GROUP OF HOTELS

Garden House Hotel, Tel 096 756995, Fax (01) 233264
Email: gardengroup@zamtel.zm
Web: www.zambiatourism.com/gardengroup, Located on the Mumbwa road.

Kafue Road Garden Motel
Tel (097) 792738/ 097 825700,
Kafue Rd Makeni,
Email: gardengroup@zamtel.zm
Website: www.zambiatourism.com/gardengroup

Margarets Guest House
Tel (01) 295356 (096)760527
Fax (01) 295356
Plot 62 Luwato Road Roma

Margaret's Guesthouse

Musuma Garden Guest House
Tel (01) 294470 /294125,
Fax (01)291887,
220 Mutandwa Rd, Roma,
Email: lq@zamnet.zm
Web: www.leisurequest.co.zm,
Guest house offering conference facilities for smaller groups

Musuma Garden
Accommodation & Conference venue

Anina's Guest House
Tel (01) 227413/ 279045/ (097) 848662,
Fax (01) 223373,
Plot 29b Lilayi Road, Lilayi,
Email: sondashi@zamnet.zm,
Comfortable rooms with basic amenities.

Cha Cha Cha Backpackers
Telefax (01) 222257,
Mulobwa close, Fairview
Email: cha@zamtel.zm
Well-established and good place for budget travellers. Not fancy but relaxed feel and owners great source of information. Dorms, singles, doubles, tents also available. Close to town.

Chainama Hotel, Tel (01) 292451/ 292450, Fax (01) 290809, Great East Rd
Email: chahotel@zamnet.zm
Located on the Great East Road with comforatable rooms and basic amenities.

Countrywood Lodge
Tel (006) 758902
Njuka Road, Olympia
Comfortable rooms in pleasant surroundings with basic amenities.

Eureka Camp Site, Tel (01) 275491
Fax (01) 225491, Off Kafue Road, Lilayi
Email: eureka@zamnet.zm
Set on small private game farm with pleasant grounds. Ideal for travellers and overnight stops. Offers chalets and camping with bar and restaurant.

Fairview Hotel, Tel (01) 239741
Fax (01) 239741, Church Road
Located near the city centre, basic amenities meeting room facilities.

Classic Hospitality

PEARL HAVEN INN

"The Pearl in the City"

Welcome to Lusaka's premier guest house and lodge. Situated in the heart of Lusaka, within walking distance of Manda Hill Shopping Centre, Pearl Haven Inn is the ideal travellers or businessman's retreat. Relax at our well stocked bar or cool off in the pool. One is always met with a warm, welcoming smile from our highly qualified and trained staff. Sample the tastiest cuisine in town prepared the way you want it. Our airconditioned rooms are self-contained and have DSTV and direct dailing telephones.

COURTESY VEHICLE AVAILABLE TO AND FROM THE AIRPORT.

Room rates:

US$60 a day - single

US$80 a day - double

US$90 a day - twin or deluxe

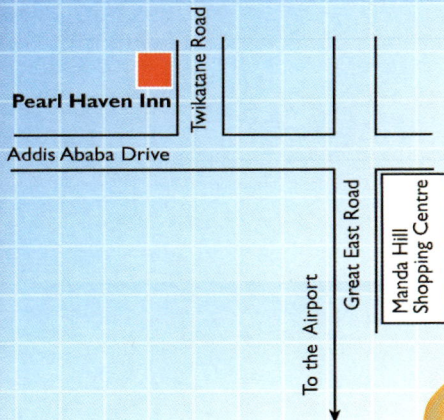

Twikatane Road

Pearl Haven Inn

Addis Ababa Drive

To the Airport

Great East Road

Manda Hill Shopping Centre

For reservations, contact:
5 Twikatane Road, Rhodes Park
P.O. Box 50109 Lusaka
Tel: 252412 / 252455 Fax: 251126
E-mail: pearl@zamnet.zm
www.pearlhaven.co.zm

GARDEN GROUP OF HOTELS

HEAD OFFICE: NDEKE HOTEL
P.O. BOX 30815 LUSAKA 10101 ZAMBIA
TEL: 00 260 1 251734 FAX: 00 260 1 233264
E-mail: gardengroup@zamtel.zm
Website:www.zambiatourism.com/gardengroup

Ndeke Hotel Longacres Lusaka

A family hotel with cocktail bar, restaurant and swimming pool, 44 rooms ensuite and 2 suites.
We organise workshops, cocktail parties,
Borad meetings and outside catering on request.
For prices contact: Patrick Mwaanga on 251734
Kris Nyalugwe on 096-750900

Leisure Bay Lodge

P.O. Box 68 Siavonga.
20 rooms ensuite almost all facing the lake
Pleasant surroundings, Cocktail bar, swimming
Pool under construction. Special prices for weekends.
Specialises in meetings, workshops and seminars. Contact:
Gibson Phiri on 096-765259
Or Mr Mbewe on 511136

Kafue Road Garden

P.O. Box 30815 Lusaka
Situated on the Kafue Road opposite the Castle Shopping Centre. Popular Hotel for workshops, seminars, weddings and cocktail parties.
The Hotel has 22 twin rooms, cocktail bar and restaurant, function room from 10 to 120 people. Prices on request.
Contact: Andrew Chomba on 097-792738
Or Derrick Ngwira on 097-825700
Reception: 097-828771

Garden House Hotel

50 ensuite rooms set out on extensive gardens, swimming pool. Workshops and seminars, weddings and cocktail parties. The hotel has 7 function rooms catering for parties from 10 to 150 People.
Outside catering and industrial catering available on request.
Contact: 01-233004
096-756995

Handsen's Lodge, Tel (01) 292734/ 225238, Fax (01) 225243, Plot 9694 Off Munali road, Chudleigh
Basic amenities, also offering business and secretarial facilities.

Endesha Guest House, Tel (01) 225780 Fax (01) 225781, Perinenyatwa road
Near town, clean, friendly, good value.

Makeni Guest House, Tel (01) 274667 Makeni road
Email: jkazunga@zamnet.zm
Basic facilities.

Millennium Lodge
Tel (01) 260717/096 453825
Fax (01) 263977, Plot 5 Reedbuck Rd, Kabulonga, Email: milo@millennum.zm
Pleasant surroundings, swimming pool.

Mumana Pleasure Resort
Telefax (01) 291011
Great East Road
Located on the airport road.

Mumana Lodge
Tel (01) 291860
Fax (01) 291863, Olympia Extension
Email: mumana@zamnet.zm
Basicamenities.

Oleander Lodge, Tel (01) 284215 /096 759792
55 Oleander road, Avondale
Basic amenities.

Oriental Gardens
Tel (01) 293574/097803337
United Nations Avenue
Comfortable rooms and a good restaurant.

Pioneer Campsite
Tel (096) 432700 /437366
2.5km east from the Airport turnoff, Palabana Road
Email: 2pioneer@bushmail.net
Website: www.pioneercampzambia.com
Good value and well-run. Camping offered under big shady trees. Meals and self catering kitchen with fully stocked bar.

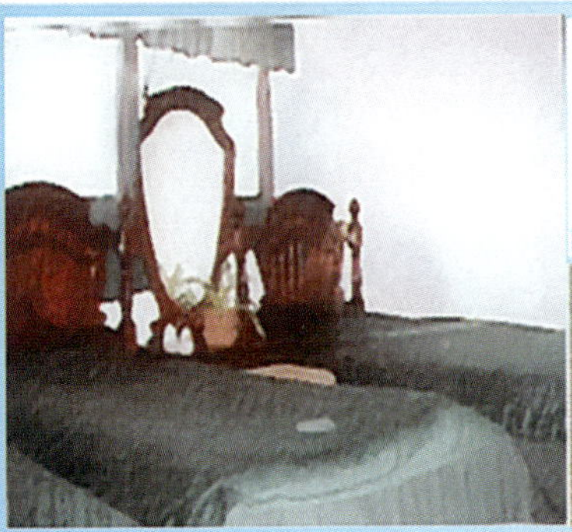

Village Rest, Tel 096 439419,
Fax (01) 241311
Off Kafue Road, Lilayi
Email: mtz@zamnet.zm
Ideal stop over for travellers; thatched bar & restaurant next to pool. Set in nice open lawns. Clean and comfortable.

Vineyard lodge
Tel (01) 291204
Plot 6610, Mumana Road,
Olympia Extension
Email: vineyard@zamnet.zm
Luxurious double rooms, tastefully decorated with local articrafts.

Wila's Lodge, Tel (01) 238402/ 097 809238 , Fax (01) 237841
Email: wilalodge@zamnet.zm
Basic facilities.

Wayside Bed & Breakfast
Tel (01) 273439, Fax (01) 274444
Makeni Road.
Basic amenities.

Welcome Home Guesthouse
Tel (01) 293574 /097 803337
Fax (01) 293574, Plot 441a Lukanga Road, Roma
Email:usoko@zamtel.zm
Basic amenities

Outside Lusaka

Within easy access of the capital there are a number of attractive places to stay, notably Chaminuka which is a private game reserve and can be accessed from the International Airport or the Great North Road.

Chaminuka
Tel (01) 213303/4,
Fax (01) 213305
Email:infomation@chaminuka.com
Web: www.chaminuka.com
Hosts a private art collection with the largest collection of paintings and sculptures of the master artists of Zamba including unique African artefacts.

Real
African Wilderness
in all its magnificence

one hour from the Lusaka City Centre -

30 minutes from the airport

CHAMINUKA

Nature Reserve

Elephant, Giraffe, Lion, Cheetah, Hyena, Zebra,

every type of Antelope, Ostrich and a spectacular variety

of Birds, Pristine Miombo Woodland and Savannah.

Refined Lodge, Friendly hosts, the largest Art Collection

and the best Food in Zambia.

The Place on the Hill

Goman Ogilvy & Mather

Chisamba Protea

Tel (095) 704600/1/2/3,
Fax (095) 704800,
Email: chisamba@zamnet.zm
Web: www.proteahotels.com.
Set within a private game ranch, excellent conference facilities set in tranquil surroundings with thatched cottages. 30 minutes from Lusaka on the Geat North Rd, well signposted.

Ibis Gardens

Tel (01) 233764/233766/096 754086, Fax (01) 233764
Email: Ibis@zamnet.zm
Midway between Lusaka and Kabwe, conference facilities available.

Fringilla Guest House

Tel (01) 611199, Fax (01) 611213
Email: fingill@zamnet.zm,
Small village set-up with a post office, bank, butchery, tailoring, carpentry, school and shop. Farm hospitality atmosphere with children's play ground. Offers a variety of accommodation and conferance facilities.

Lechwe Lodge

Tel 095 704 803 /097 879401,
Fax (032) 30707
Email: kflechwe@zamnet.zm
Only one hour's drive from Lusaka on the floodplains of the Kafue River, lovely accommodation with a wide range of activities. Well signposted from Kafue town.

Adventure City

A few kilometres from town on Leopard's Hill road opposite the American School is a recreation centre in extensive gardens offering numerous activities.

Great place for kids, big waterslides, a number of swimming pools where you can swim or play games. Also relaxing place for braais. Tel (096) 860018

Animal Sanctuary and Botanical gardens

Botanical garden sanctuary park located on the road to Kafue in Chilanga with a growing number of animals including lions and African wild dogs, also with beautiful botanical gardens called Munda Wanga.

Tel (01) 278456, Fax (01) 278529,
Kafue Rd, Chilanga,
Email: biopark@zamnet.zm

Art Galleries

African Gallery, Tel (01) 271202
Fax (01) 293750, Off Central Street, Chudleigh

Gallery Gear, Tel (01) 235949
Fax (01) 239420, Joseph Mwila Rd, Rhodes Park, *Email: gbcross@zamnet.zm*
Specialised picture framing with adjacent gallery where you can buy typical Zambian scenic views.

Henry Tayali Gallery, Tel (01) 254526
Showgrounds, Off Great East Rd
Ongoing exhibitions of paintings by Masters and up-coming Zambian artists available here.

Namwandwe Gallery
Tel (01) 260459
Off Leopards Hill Road
Email: www.namwandwe.bizland.com
A private gallery, set in an architecurally impressive building in a tranquil setting, hosting a contemporary gallery with paintings and sculptures of the Master artists in Zambia.

Nsolo Gallery, Tel (097) 883567
Off Tito road
Email: lukugems@zamnet.zm
Local handmade silver

Rockstone Art Gallery
Tel (01) 264907,
Kabulonga
Email: rockstone@zamnet.zm
A contemporary art gallery with wooden (ebony and mukwa) and stone sculptures and paintings available for sale.

Zamntambi, Tel (096) 747476
InterContinental Hotel
Promoter of Zambian artists with a permanent curated exhibition.

Books
American Centre, Comesa Building, Ben Bella Rd
Library and venue for exhibitions related to the American way of life, venue for various events.

BookCellar
Tel (01) 255475
Manda Hill Shopping Centre, Bookshop
Good selection of travel books.

Book World, Tel (01) 255470
Manda Hill Shopping Centre and Cairo Rd

British Council Library
Tel (01) 223602, 228332, Cairo Rd, British Council Bldg Heroes Place
Email: info@britishcouncil.org.zm
Library and venue for exhibitions related to British way of life, venue for various events.

Planet Books
Tel (01) 256715, Arcades Mall

Mary's Bookshop
Tel (01) 222114/
096 767704 , Fax (01) 226694
Leopards Hill Rd
Secondhand bookshop.

Bowling
10 Pin Bowling at Arcades Mall, adjacent to the Cinema.

Cinemas
Ster Kinekor, Tel (01) 256726
Located at Arcades Mall

Metro
Located at Avondale shopping complex, off Great East road

Cultural Centre
Kabwata Cultural Village, Burma Rd, Kabwata, Art & Crafts

A village in the heart of Lusaka, which puts on traditional dances and events. A good place to buy crafts. It was built in the 1930s and 1940s by the colonial government, and once had more than 300 huts. After independence most of the huts were demolished and the remaining 43 form what is today known as Kabwata cultural village. Currently the villagers, government and private sector are working together to improve the facilities

Farms
There are a number of well stocked game farms close to the city, where you stay overnight or enjoy a day of good food, drink and a game drive. These include Lilayi Lodge, Lechwe Lodge, Chisamba Lodge and Chaminuka, which boasts one of the largest and most interesting African art collections in Zambia, see places to stay for contact details(pages 104-106).

About 25km east of Lusaka lies Kalimba Reptile Farm, which has a large snake collection and some highly unusual chameleons. There's also a garden, children's playground and refreshment area.

KALIMBA
REPTILE PARK
Tel (01) 213272 / 095 753261,
Fax (01) 213272
Email: kalimba@zamnet.zm
Farm 4065, Ngwerere Reptile farm

Fox Dale Ostrich farm, Tel (01) 290579, Fax (01) 293838, also offering birdwatching. **Lazy J Farm,** Tel (01) 230710, Leopards Hill road. Horse riding trails, polo cross and walking. **Trotover Equestrian Centre**, Tel (01) 223014, Fax (01) 263607. Just outside of town on Leopards Hill road, offers riding lessons and hacking through the bush, lovely woodland for walks.

Golf Clubs

Chainama Hills Golf Club
Tel (01) 251010, Along Kamloops Rd Sports Club.

Chilanga Golf Club, Chilanga.

Lusaka Golf Club , Tel (01) 251598/ 250244, Los Angeles Boulevard Rd.

Marina

Located on the Kafue River about 50km south of Lusaka, the Kafue Marina is a popular weekend retreat for picnics and boating. No swimming.

National Museum

Good exhibition of contemporary artists downstairs, while upstairs, there's a delight of interesting objects which gives an insight into Zambian traditional life. Tel (01) 228807, off Independence Avenue, Kamwala

Night Life

Browns, Tel (01) 221352, Kabelenga Rd Night Club/pub.

Chez Ntemba, Wamulwa Rd,Thornpark Rhumba Night Club.

The Country Club
Off the Kafue road after Baobab School.

Engineers Pub
Located in Central Park off Cairo Road.

Johnnys
Tel (097) 771212, Lagos Road, Rhodes Park.

The HQ, Great East road, Northmead Shopping Centre
Mature Night Club.

The Jab Sports Bar
Located at Castle shopping centre, Kafue road.

Times Cafe
Located at Arcades Mall, Great East road

O'Hagans
Located at Manda Hill Shopping Centre. Irish Pub.

Polo Grill
Located on Nangwenya road, Opposite the International School.

La Reference
Southend of Freedom way.
Rhumba Night Club.

Mc Gintys, Holiday Inn, Church Rd
Irish theme pub and restaurant, high prices, offering pub food.

Majestic Casino & Restaurant
Kafue Road, Makeni.

Xenon Night Club
Northmead Shopping Centre off Great East Rd, Night Club

Debonairs, Tel: (01) 255577-9
Fax: (01) 255580
Email: msuri@coppernet.zm
Fast food pizza outlet located at Manda Hill shopping centre & Kabulonga

Steers, Tel: (01) 255577 /264069, Fax: (01) 251518, *Email: msuri@coppernet.zm*
Fast food outlet, burgers, sandwiches, icecream. Situated at Manda Hill Shopping Centre & Kabulonga

Mr. Pete's Steakhouse
Tel: (01) 223428
Plot 1664 Panganani Rd
Email: mrpetes@zamnet.zm
Restaurant/Pub specialises in spare ribs & steaks

Dil Restaurant
Tel: (01) 262391
Fax: (01) 222655, 253
Ibex Hill Rd, Kabulonga,
Email: astro@zamnet.zm
Good quality Indian dishes, with plenty of choice for vegetarians.

Fragigi, Tel: (01) 255492, Located at Manda Hill
Email: fgigi@coppernet.zm
Speciality Italian restaurant and coffee shop open till late

Giant Dragon
Tel: (01) 263893 /265861 Kabulonga road, Chinese restaurant, excellent cuisine, good ambience.

Johnnys, Tel (097) 771212, Lagos rd. Rhodes Park. Chinese, Malaysian and selected Indian dishes. Pub atmoshere.

Marlin Resturant
Tel: (01) 252206/096 765462,
Fax: (01) 252184, At the
Lusaka Club, Los Angeles
Boulevard
Email: vencat@coppernet.zm
Best steak in town, wonderful pepper
sauce. Reservations crucial for evenings.

Piccolo

Piccolo, Tel: (01) 261316/261322/
096 762445. Located on Serval road, off
Middleway, Kabulonga.
Haute cuisine

Premuni

Premuni Restaurant
Tel: (01) 224209
Plot 61 Great East Road
Email: sunetabhanderi@hotmail.com
Restaurant serving authentic Indian cuisine specializing in vegetarian dishes.

Cattleman's Grill, Tel: (01) 253606
Chrismar Hotel, Los Angeles Boulevard
Steak restaurant and pub, open 24hrs.

Chang Shuan, Tel: (01) 252654
Fax: (01) 252654, Independence Avenue
Chinese cuisine

Chit Chat Café, Tel: (01) 294264
Omelo Mumba road, Rhodes Park
Café/coffee shop.
Set in lovely garden, good for children.

Danny's Restaurant & Memories of China
Tel: (01) 253787, Haile Selassie Avenue,
Longacres.
Specialising in Indian and Chinese cuisine.

Dong Fang, Tel: (01) 250375
Chisidza road, off Los Angeles Boulevard
Offers a wide selection of Chinese food
and at good prices.

El Toro Coffee Shop, Tel: (01) 263272
Sable road, Kabulonga
Selection of good home cooking and confectionary.

GIANT DRAGON RESTAURANT
Specialised in Cantonese Cuisine
Open 7 days a week (Lunch & Dinner)

Tel: 263893 / 265861 Kabulonga Road, Lusaka

Manda Hill Shopping Centre
Kabulonga Shopping Centre

We Deliver Smartly
Manda Hill Shopping Centre - Tel: 255578/79
Kabulonga Shopping Centre - Tel: 264069

Engineers Pub, Tel: (01) 223445
Central Park, Cairo road
Nice pub atmosphere, small but interesting menu and good service, worth a visit.

Food Fayre, Tel: (01) 238470,
Cairo road & Arcades Mall
Fast food outlet.

Garden Tea Shop, Lusaka Showgrounds
Home to the garden society of Zambia.
Coffee shop with lovely small garden.

Gerritz, Tel: (01) 253639, Chaholi road,
Off Addis Ababa Drive
Pleasant, colourful Mexican décor, option to eat in or out. Unusual dishes, German chef keen on different sauces.

Hibiscus, Tel: (01) 295011
Fax: (01) 291657, Central Street,
Jesmodine
Cordon bleu French/Belgium cuisine.
Reservations recommended.

LA Fast Food, Tel: (01) 251285
Haile Selassie Avenue, Longacres
Fast food outlet, chicken, pizzas, and restaurant on the first floor.

La Patisserie, Tel: (01) 224008
Fax: (01) 224097, Central Park,
Cairo road
Coffee shop with great bakery, good pies and sandwiches.

Le Triumph Dolphin, Tel: (01) 292133
Paseli road, Northmead
Seafood and Creole Specialities with live entertainment on Friday nights.

Musuku Restaurant, Tel: (01) 251666
Holiday Inn, Church road
Continental cuisine

O' Hagans, Tel: (01) 255555, Manda Hill
Shopping Centre, Great East road
Irish-style pub and restaurant specialising in Irish food, large portions.

Olive Grove, Tel: (01) 250600
Hotel InterContinental,
Haile Selassie Avenue.
Mediterranean restaurant, overlooking the swimming pool.

Oriental Gardens, Tel: (01) 252163
Fax: (01) 255719,United Nations Avenue
Well priced, good Indian cuisine, opposite the American Embassy.

Polo Grill, Nangwenya road,
Rhodes Park
Relaxed, open air venue overlooking the polo field, good place for sundowners.

Sichuan, Tel: (01) 253842, Showgrounds
Good Chinese cuisine, special hot sauce.

Spice Paradise, Tel: (01) 262078
Kabulonga road
Superb Indian food at good prices

Steaks & Grills, Tel: (01) 254455
Taj Pamodzi Hotel, Church road.
Grill restaurant. International & Indian cuisine.

Subway, Tel: (01) 255580, Manda Hill
Centre, Great East road and Arcades.
Fast food sandwich outlet with a wide variety of fillings to choose from.

Life tastes good

Coca-Cola

SHOPPING

Catering to avowedly up market locals, *Manda Hill Shopping Centre* is one of Lusaka's favourite hangouts. This shopping centre has a number of fast food outlets, department stores, boutiques, beauty salons, banks and curio outlets. Down the road from Manda Hill is *Arcades Entertainment Centre*, a new shopping Mall with a first multi-screen cinema, ten pin bowling alley and a large variety of restaurants. Lusaka's other main shopping areas include Northmead, where there's a small but nice market, Kabulonga and Longacres. A modern glass building called *Central Park* on the north end of Cairo Road which combines business and retail outlets in one place, La Patisserie coffee shop where you can get good croissants, cappuccino and pies, and the very good Engineers Pub.

Places to Shop

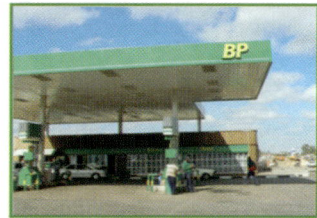

115

MANDA HILL CENTER

Centre Management

Tel: 255550   Fax: 255551

E-mail:
mandahill@zamnet.zm
mandahill@zamtel.zm

Banks and Money Exchange

Barclays Bank	255472
Standard Chartered Bank	255483/4
Stero Bureau De Change	255765
Zambia National Commercial Bank	255524/7

Departmental Stores and Supermarkets

Game Stores	255450
Pep Stores	255512
Shoprite Checkers	251155
	255410
	255401
Smart Centre	255517/8
Truworths	255162
W Stores	255129

Electronics and Hi-Fi

Hi-Fi and Electric City	255466
Philips Radian Stores	255161

Furniture

Barnetts	255535 -40
Batex	255319
Carnival	255562-64
Ellerines	255674

Fashion

Abeve Quality Centre	255697
Guys and Girls	255568
Kool teens	255681
Petauke Place	255489
What's New Boutique	255507

Hair and Beauty

Salon Namel	255513

Hardware

Handyman's Paradise	255781

Jewellery

Klaus Rygaard Jewellers	255477-8

Kiddies Fashion

Baby Boom	255565
Les Petit Elegants	255567

Medical Services

Link Pharmacy	255556
Medicare Opticians	255480

Music

Sounds Investment	255570

Photographic

Phoenix Photo	255469

Pottery and Tiles

Moore Pottery	255479

Restaurants/Beverages/Confectionary

Douglas and Tate	255558
Fragigi	255492
Gingerbread Cottage	096 7672
Hungry Lion	255514
Nando's / Creamy inn / Chicken Inn	252773
O'Hagan Irish Pub	255555
Steers / Blockbusters /Debonairs	255580/1
	255577/9
Subway Sandwiches	255569
Vasillis	252773

Sewing and Needlecraft

Needles and Craft	255548

Shoes and Accessories

Bata	255326
Denary Footwear	251606
Lexort Leather	255078
	255071
Multiserv	255571

Specialists Services, Agencies and Shops

Post.net	255546
ZESCO	258309
	254884
Homenet Real Estate	255747
Celtel	255661
Telecel	096 750030

Stationery, Gifts and Books

Bookcellar	255475/6
Bookworld	255470
Reflections	255560

Sports Shops

Reebok Sports	255495

EVERYTHING UNDER THE SUN

Manda Hill Centre
Tel (01) 255550,
Fax (01) 255551,
Great East Rd
Email: mandahill@zamnet.zm
Shopping mall, with a variety of shops

Lusaka International Community School
Tel 01 292447/290626
242A, Kakola Rd, Roma
Email: lics@coppernet.zm
Website: www.lics.sch.zm

Sub Zero Electronics
Tel (01) 225347, Stand 2 Cairo road
Email: sub0@zamnet.zm

Cascades
Tel: 262992, Sable road, Kabulonga
Fresh vegetables with home industries.

Jagoda Enterprises
Tel (01) 223131, Fax (01) 223131
Buyantashi road, Rhodes Park
Lovely gemstones set in silver and gold.

Klaus Rygaard
Tel (01) 255277/8
Manda Hill Centre, Great East road
Pure Zambian silver and gem stones at competitive prices.

Moore Pottery
Tel 097 843403, Kabelenga road
Manufacturers of locally designed pottery, wrought iron and beadwork.

Savannah Wood
Tel (01) 261032/ 097 882750,
Fax (01) 261032
Kabulonga road, opposite Kabulonga Girls School.
Quality furniture made from reclaimed railway sleepers.

Markets

Lusaka has a number of markets but **Soweto** is the biggest and most famous in the country. It is a place where you can buy everything from second hand Calvin Klein shirts to traditional herbal medicines. Consists of a large covered market bordered by a sprawling collection of stalls and bus station, this teeming, vibrant and colourful market should only be visited by the more adventurous. Don't carry valuables and don't photograph people without asking.

Tuesday Vegetable Market
Burma Road, Kabwata
Fresh farm vegetables, every Tuesday.

Northmead Market, Great East road
Stalls selling wooden carvings, basketwork and vegetables.

Monthly Craft Market at the Dutch Reformed Church, Kabulonga road
A bustling market where you can get good quality, home-made goods, including African fabrics, sculptures, baskets, as well as antiques (though watch out for the fakes). Takes place on the last Saturday of every month. Within grounds are small but charming coffee shop. The Bancroft Garden, where you can also buy plants and Savannah Wood.

OVATION 6658

Let's talk
about your personal
e-mail connection.

Celtelplus Mobile e-mail is another Value Added Service from Celtel, Africa's most advanced cellular phone network. It gives you a free e-mail address - so wherever you take your phone, you will have access to the internet to exchange e-mails with friends, family and your contacts throughout the world.

As another Celtel Value Added Service, Celtelplus Mobile e-mail is yours **FREE*** of charge, as soon as you get connected to the Celtel network.

For more information dial 111 FREE from your mobile phone and let's talk.

* E-mail set-up and address is free, but airtime charges of 15 cents per minute apply when using the service.
CELTEL HQ Celtel House, Box 320001, Nyerere Road, Woodlands, Lusaka. Tel: 260 1 250707 or Toll Free 111 from your mobile phone. Fax: 260 1 250595. **KITWE OFFICE** 9 Mpezeni Way, Box 20768, Kitwe. Tel: 260 2 232423. Fax: 260 2 232422. **LIVINGSTONE OFFICE**. Shop Number 952, Musi O Tunya Road, Box 61161. Tel 260 3 320660. Fax: 260 3 320658. **KABWE OUTLET**. Shop No. 19 Independence Way, Kabwe. **MANDA HILL OUTLET**. Shop No. 35, Manda Hill Centre, Great East Road. Tel: 260 1 255661. Customer Care: 260 97 770066. **CAIRO ROAD OUTLET**. Plot 17/18 Grand House, Cairo Road South End, Lusaka.

Celtel
Let's talk.

VICTORIA FALLS & LIVINGSTONE

For first-time visitors to Zambia, the sights and thrills of the Victoria Falls or Mosi-o-Tunya, one of the world's greatest natural wonders, and the country's tourist capital of Livingstone are a must.

There's a good reason why even seasoned travellers keep coming back for more – there's a huge amount to do and see whatever your taste and Victoria Falls' reputation as the adrenaline centre of Southern Africa is well earned. The nearby town of Livingstone has emerged out of its slumber and decay to become a lively place without losing the laid-back atmosphere of its colonial past.

Named after the Scottish missionary and explorer, David Livingstone, the former colonial capital is a living reminder of the years of British rule. It is full of charming public buildings with wide steps, columned entrances and white facades. Edwardian residences and Cape Dutch churches evoke an atmosphere of a bygone age. But its atmosphere is also very much African.

Founded in 1905 after the abandonment of an earlier settlement at the Old Drift, the new healthier site had many advantages. In 1911 Livingstone became the capital of the new Northern Rhodesia colony but when in 1935 Lusaka took over as the administrative centre Livingstone had to find a new role for itself. By the time of Zambia's independence in the 1960s, it had carved out a niche as the tourist capital of Zambia, thanks to the magnificent Victoria Falls. In 2005 Livingstone will be celebrating the centenary of the city and 150 years since David Livingstone first discovered the falls. Today Livingstone is one of Africa's most enjoyable holiday centres, complete with international airport.

The Victoria Falls are 11km from Livingstone. One of the seven natural wonders of the world, the Victoria Falls are the greatest curtain of falling water on earth and sometimes the spray can be seen up to 80kms away.

The clouds of spray and tremendous roar produced by this immense amount of water, crashing down into a narrow chasm, gave rise to its more exotic African name, Mosi-o-Tunya, translated as 'the smoke that thunders'.

The Victoria Falls, 1,708 metres wide and 103 metres deep at their highest point, are in fact divided into six waterfalls: Devils Cataract, Main Falls, Horseshoe Falls, Rainbow Falls, Armchair Falls and the Eastern Cataract. Around them are a rich tropical rainforest, watered by the moisture of the spray. For centuries these dazzling waterfalls were considered to be sacred and local people came here to pray and make their offerings. Only following the visit of David Livingstone in 1855 did they come to the attention of the Western world. Soon they became an integral part of the grand African tour for the adventurous and wealthy. However, only with the explosion of air travel have more people been able to view them. Zambia and Zimbabwe, which share the Falls, have taken measures to protect the area surrounding the Falls and today it is a UNESCO-designated World Heritage site.

THE CITY OF LIVINGSTONE

To Livingstone International Airport

Wasawange Hotel

LUSAKA ROAD
WATER TOWER
ZAMBEZI SPORTS CLUB

ELAINE BRITTEL

Chanter's Restaurant

Grubby's Grotto

OBTE AVE

KATETE AVE

HATEKE ROAD

MARAMBA

Maloke Lodge

GWEMBE STREET

Fairmont Hotel

SCHOOL LANE
MUSHU WAY
NEHRU WAY
MWELA WAY
MWELA WAY

ZAMNET

CHIMWEMWE WAY

Curios

PETROL

SHAFIK'S CLINIC

Zig Zag Cafe

LIVINGSTONE HOSPITAL

Immigrations

NORTHWEST HOTEL

BATOKA HOSPITAL

MAAMBO WAY

LUKUI STREET

Buses

OFFICE OF THE PRESIDENT

POST OFFICE

BANKS

MAPELWA WAY

POLICE

MARAMBA ROAD

MARAMBA MARKET

GANDHI AVE.

CHISAMBA RD.

Livingstone Museum

SHOPRITE SUPERMARKET

WAR MEMORIAL

PRISON

TAXIS

CENTRAL MARKET

HINDU HALL

ARCHITECTURE STUDIOS

LIVINGSTONE GOLF COURSE

MARAMBA RIVER

TOURIST INFO & ZNTB

KANYETA RD.

MOSI-OA-TUNYA HOUSE

PETROL

Jollyboys Backpackers

NYERERE ROAD

TANZANIA ROAD

BUSIKU CLUB

KAPUFI AVENUE

MAHA AVE.

CIVIC CENTRE

The Mission Backpackers

CONVENT WAY

SAKANDA ROAD

CHITEMBO ROAD

LINDA ROAD

Pig's Head Pub

FIRE STATION

PETROL

KABOMPO ROAD

MOSI-OA-TUNYA ROAD

CATHOLIC CHURCH

Jet Extreme

NYASA ROAD

LINDA

SPORTS GROUND

CEMETERY

DAVID LIVINGSTONE HIGH SCHOOL

TOUCH ADVENTURES

Hippo's Restaurant

PETROL

TWO SEVENTEEN

KUSTE ROAD

To up-river lodges and Kazungula Botswana border

NKUMBI ROAD

NAKATINDI ROAD

CAR HIRE

Fawlty Towers Backpackers

ADVENTURE CENTRE
CRAFT & CURIO SHOP

Jungle

VET

Internet

ACTIVE LINK BUSINESS AND TOURIST INFO

FINTA DAIRIES

AFRICAN VISIONS ART & CRAFT GALLERY

The Zambezi Swing

GREGOS

BUSHTRACKS

DAMBWA

drawn by Peter Jones ©

NSANSA ROAD

BRIGHT SERVICES
ZAMBIAN BREWERIES

Funkey Munkey Restaurant

COIN SECURITY

NATIONAL MILLING CO.

KAFUBU ROAD

RAILWAY STATION

CHISAMBA FALLS ROAD

LIMULUNGA ROAD

To the Victoria Falls & Zimbabwe border

Ngolide Lodge

Customs

Gecko's Backpackers

CHISAMBA FALLS ROAD
RAILWAY MUSEUM

Peter Jones

MOSI-O-TUNYA (VICTORIA FALLS)

On 16 November 1855, when David Livingstone first saw the waterfalls known as Mosi-o-Tunya, or 'The Smoke That Thunders', he was so captivated that he renamed them Victoria Falls in honour of his sovereign, Queen Victoria. This was the one and only time Livingstone bestowed a name of his own choice rather than retaining the indigenous name.

Mosi-o-Tunya was the name given to the Falls by the Makololo. The Makololo were a tribe of formidable warriors who broke free from Shaka Zulu's empire in South Africa and migrated to this area in the 1830s. They conquered this area, but after a period of almost twenty-five years were overthrown. One of the reminders of their brief period of rule is this apt and beautiful name. The earlier name given by the Toka Leya, Shungu Namutitima, which also means 'the smoke that thunders' has never gained wide usage.

The Falls are constantly changing character depending on the time of day, the weather and the season. In fact the local Toka Leya people have a number of names for the Falls, depending on the season.

To appreciate and understand all its moods, the Victoria Falls should be visited not once but many times. When the Zambezi river is at its highest between February and June, up to 10 million litres per second plunge over the precipice and even in the dry season, between September and November, when the flow of water is drastically reduced, up to a million litres of water per second cascade over.

In the dry season, it is much easier to see and appreciate the geological history of the Falls. Because almost no water plunges over the Eastern Cataract, it is possible to walk across the basalt to Livingstone Island. It is from this island that David Livingstone, having descended the river by canoe, got his first view of the Victoria Falls in 1855. But be warned, it's now a private island, operated by one of the safari companies, and so you may not be allowed on.

In the months when water flow is at its height (March - June), spray is so dense that you may not get a good view of the Falls and you will get utterly soaked. This is all part of the thrill, but be careful with cameras.

Visiting the Falls in the early morning and late afternoons is highly recommended because of the softness of the light, perfect for capturing the Fall's famous rainbow.

If you're around at the time of the full moon, take advantage of the extended opening times of the park grounds. There's nothing quite as magical as a lunar rainbow.

There can be few experiences on this earth so gratifying and exhilarating as watching the gushing white waters of the magnificent Victoria Falls. The experience is made all the more thrilling by the fact that, unlike many other waterfalls around the world, it is possible to get right up close and walk right in front of the Falls. Just be careful!

Well-kept paths lead to different viewing spots. One of the most astonishing views is from the Knife Edge

Bridge. This is as close as you will get to the Falls. This bridge, which was built in 1969 by the Zambian government, spans a narrow ridge of rock between the mainland and island downstream opposite the Eastern Cataract.

It's the best and most hair-raising way of seeing the Rainbow Falls, Main Falls, the first Gorge and the Boiling Pot.

Another main vantage point is the famous 650 ft-long Victoria Falls railway bridge which spans the deep Batoka Gorge and links Zambia with Zimbabwe.

For a complete impression, cross over the border to see the Falls from the Zimbabwe side.

The trip is easy and quick, but make sure the officials know that you are travelling simply to view the Falls so that your visa is not affected.

PETER JONES ©

ZAMBIA

LIVINGSTONE CITY

Mosi - Oa - Tunya
National Park

Mosi - Oa - Tunya
National Park

LIVINGSTONE CITY AND THE VICTORIA FALLS

ZIMBABWE

VIC FALLS TOWN

SINDE RIVER

ZAMBEZI RIVER

MARAMBA RIVER

MARAMBA

LUNDA

HANSANSU RIVER

SONGWE RIVER

NORTH

MARAMBA RIVER

CATARACT PARK

Livingstone Island

SILOKA ISLAND

RAILWAY MUSEUM

SILUNGU MUFU

OLD DRIFT CEMETERY

BATOKA GORGE

LOOKOUT TREE

LOOKOUT TREE

Wasawange Hotel

Livingstone International Airport

Lobengula's Rest

Susi & Choma Lodge

Thorntree Lodge

Tongabezi

River Club

Zoological Park

Microlite Flips

Nyala Lodge

Pete's Steak House

River Shack

The Zambezi Waterfront

Taonga Boat Club

Crocodile Park

Maramba River Lodge

Helicopter Flips

Sun International Hotels

Lost Horizons

Stanley Safari Lodge

ZAMBIAN BORDER POST

111m Bungi Jump

White Water Rafting

Kayaking

Riverboarding

Jet Boats

The Gorge Swing

TO CHIEF MUKUNI'S VILLAGE
SONGWE VILLAGE AND
TAITA FALCON LODGE

ROAD TO KAZANGULA
AND BOTSWANA

ROAD TO VIC FALLS
AIRPORT AND TO
BULAWAYO

Zambia is the birthplace of adventure activities around the Victoria Falls, though larger commercial operators on the Zimbabwean side dominated until the recent and unfortunate decline in tourism due to the country's political turmoil. There's still a lot of overlapping with the companies.

Bungee jumping off the railway bridge, microlighting over the Victoria Falls, abseiling in the gorges, horse riding in the forests, fishing on the upper Zambezi, rafting downstream or a combination, the so-called 'combo' are some of the adventures offered by operators in the area.

You can book activities directly or through an agency, otherwise all the hotels, camp sites and backpacker lodges can book activities for you and advise on the best companies and special deals. You're not likely to get ripped off - prices for the same activities are fairly standard – just make sure you know exactly what you're paying for.

Flight of Angels

For an unsurpassed view of the famous waterfalls and the Zambezi River rapids, just above and below the Falls, take to the air in a helicopter or light wing aircraft.

Or even more exhilarating, take a microlight flight where the only thing between you and the Falls is a seat. The pilot takes photos of you and the Falls. Flights cost approximately US$70 for 15 mins, about US$115 for 30 mins. Operators are Batoka Sky, Bush Birds Flying Adventure, Del-Air, Southern Cross Aviation, United Air Services and Zambezi Helicopter Company.

White-water Rafting

Victoria Falls' reputation as the adrenaline centre of Africa started with white water rafting. The Zambezi's standing as one of the world's wildest rapids is well deserved: the 24 rapids, with grade-four and grade-five water, are huge and the Batoka Gorge, just downstream from Victoria Falls, is spectacular.

The ride will be one of the most breathtaking thrills in your life, but it's also one of the safest: Before you setoff, you'll be instructed on how to behave and react. The water is deep and the rocks too far down in the water to injure you when the boat flips, and it's likely that it will, and you have to 'swim'.

Smaller rafts take four, but the norm is seven people, with a raft guide. You can either paddle yourself through the rapids or hang on and 'highside' while the guide steers the way. It can get busy, and sometimes there are up to 20 boats on the river.

Where you start and which rapids you do depends on water levels: of course, the higher the water, the less exciting the rapids.

A day of rafting is exhausting, but save some energy for the long walk out of the gorge at the end of which awaits a much-needed cold drink. In the evening the video of the day's adventure is shown, which is available for purchase.

The main operators are Bundu Adventures, Frontier Adevntures, Safari Par Excellence (SafPar), Shearwater and Touch Adventure, some of which offer longer, highly recommended, downstream trips.

After the first hectic day of up to 10 rapids, the river calms down. In between the rapids, which seem to get even bigger downstream, you have a chance to marvel at the awe-inspiring Batoka Gorge and do a spot of game and bird viewing in an astonishing wilderness as you drift down the river. A week of river-rafting and camping in beautiful spots is an incredibly unwinding experience.

Costs for a day's trip are about $100, including equipment and lunch. Costs are similar for longer trips.

Other white-water Activities

For stomach-churning thrills, zoom down the Zambezi in a sleek and powerful jet boat, ducking in between rocks and spinning round and round. The operator is Jet Extreme and half-day, which means about one hour on the boat with up to eight passengers, costs about US$60.

Jet Extreme Ltd,
Tel (03)-321375/
263 212 655 Fax (03) 321365
12 Tanzania road , Livingstone
Email: jetextreme@zamnet.zm
Web: www.jetextreme.com
Wild water jetboating in the gorge

THE ZAMBEZI SWING

Qualified Instructors will assist you
No experience necessary
Only the best equipment is used

Set below the Victoria Falls in
the beautiful Batoka Gorges

A Full Day of unlimited: -
Gorge Swinging, Abseiling, Highwiring, Rap Jumping

A Full Day includes: -
Free Lunch, Soft Drinks & Beer, Free Visas & Transfers
Half days also available.

Book Through the Zambezi Swing office in Livingstone or Local Booking Agent

P.O. Box 61023, Livingstone - Zambia
Tel: +263 (0) 11 213835/8 or +260 (3) 321188
email: abseilzambia@hotmail.com
theswing@zamnet.zm

BECOME A MEMBER OF THE SWINGERS CLUB

ABSEIL ZAMBIA

Abseiling & Gorge Swing

Abseil Zambia operate the 'Zambezi swing' in a beautiful canyon off the main Batoka Gorge.

There are a number of options: you can leap off a 70-metre cliff on the end of a rope, expertly and safely harnessed of course; abseil, facing up or down or high-wire (which means racing along a cable on a pulley wheel).

A full day of fun, with as many attempts at whatever you like and lunch, if you have the stomach for it, costs about US$95, half day aproximately US$80.

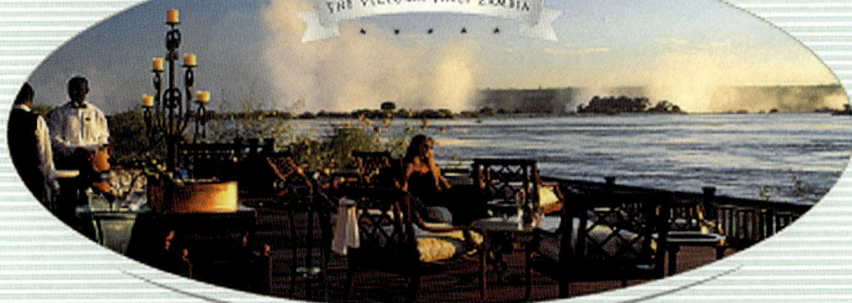

River Boarding or Surfing

If you ever want to pit yourself against the Zambezi, river boarding or surfing is the way to do it.

After learning the basic skills of catching waves in calm water, armed with only a helmet, flippers, wetsuit and body board, you head down to the gorge with a guide to take on progressively larger rapids with names like Terminator, Gnashing Jaws of Death and Stairway to Heaven.

Half-day costs about US$85, full day US$100 or so. Main operators are Serious Fun, SafPar, Bundu Adventures, Shearwater and Frontier Adventures.

Bungee Jumping

For sheer heart-stopping terror, bungee jump from the Victoria Falls bridge on the Zambezi River. At 111 metres it is one of the highest commercial bungee jumps in the world. The scenery of the gorge and the Zambezi river with the Victoria Falls as a backdrop makes the jump even more breathtaking.

Getting back on solid ground means hanging around on the end of the gigantic 'elastic band' until someone on the end of a rope winches you up to the bridge.

The operator is African Extreme. Tandem jumps, where you're strapped together with someone else, are also available, at about US$120, single jumps at US$90. A video and photos are also available for purchase.

Other activities

The natural beauty of the Zambezi is unsurpassed and a canoe trip is the best way to enjoy the upper parts of this lovely river.

This is a part of the Zambezi completely different from the white water downstream.

To relax take a sundowner cruise up the Zambezi. While gently sipping a cold drink, watch the wildlife and a gorgeous sunset over the river.

For bird-lovers, it is also possible to go on an interesting and unusual birding trip with a very professional one-man show, Bob's Birding Safaris (Tel + (263) 11 421679, Fax (03) 322224, email: bob@zamnet.zm.

A newly introduced activity is elephant back safaris offered by Thorntree River Lodge, located on Nakatindi road, offering morning or afternoon options. Tel (03) 324480, email elephants@safpar.co.zw or safpar@zamnet.zm.

Very close to the Falls and built around an actual excavation site is the Victoria Falls Field Museum, which tells the geological story of the Falls.

A few metres away is a small curio market which offers a wide range of arts and crafts, but be prepared to negotiate.

A few kilometres upstream of the Falls, with the entrance clearly marked on the road to Livingstone, is the Mosi-o-Tunya national park (admission fee of about US$3).

It's fenced, but it does feel wild, and is a really pleasant way to spend some time and see some animals. Covering about 10 square kilometres, this is the only place in Zambia where white rhinos can be seen. The white rhino is not indigenous to Zambia but was brought in from South Africa. The park also contains elephant, buffalo, zebra, sable, eland, impala, warthog, baboon and vervet monkey.

Within the national park the graves of the early Europeans settlers can be found at the Old Drift cemetery.

Most of the occupants were victims of malaria, blackwater fever and other tropical diseases. This is the only reminder of the Old Drift settlement, the first European settlement in the area, which was later abandoned in favour of the healthier site of Livingstone.

On the road to the gorges, about 18km south-east of Livingstone, is Mukuni village, a genuine African village where visitors are free to wander around, talk to people, including the artists who carve the curios for sale around the Falls.

The pressure to buy can be intense but there's no problem if you politely decline.

An influential figure, the current Chief Mukuni is a modern and enterprising man who works hard to ensure his Toka Leya people benefit from tourism and retain their traditional way of life. Visitors make donations, which go towards community projects, such as water wells and a clinic.

Tours can be arranged through hotels, travel agencies or you can make your own way there.

If you fancy more than a day in a village, you can always spend the night at Songwe Point Village, which is a few kilometres from Mukuni Village.

It's set up as a tourist village, but with some modcons. It might not suit everyone's taste, although its location is spectacular: on the edge of the Batoka gorge.

A wander around Livingstone itself as Zambia's oldest city is worthwhile. The ambience of the throb of daily African life amid old colonial buildings is pleasant.

The Livingstone Museum is also worth a visit; it's airy, well-kept and has some interesting exhibits including the archaeological section, Tonga artefacts and crafts (on sale in the shop) and David Livingstone memorabilia. In the courtyard, there's a café and paintings by Zambian artists.

If you are interested in railway history, just outside Livingstone is the Railway Museum. Among the museum exhibits are rare steam locomotives.

On the way out to the Falls is the Maramba Cultural Village puts on a great show of traditional dancing, complete with masked men on stilts.

For crafts shopping visit African Visions at the Livingstone Adventure Centre, a colourful shop with a range of quality souvenirs, fabrics, paintings and music.

Kubu crafts on Mosi-o-Tunya Road in town, which specialises in locally made furniture and associated goods and The Shop that Thunders which is right at the Falls. For local colour visit Maramba market, which sells a wide variety of goods.

One of the high points of the Zambian cultural arts scene is the Livingstone Festival with its multitude of concerts and exhibitions which includes that of painters and sculptors. For three days the whole town is dedicated to different forms of cultural expressions.

Top Range

The Royal Livingstone
Tel (03) 321122, Fax (03) 321128
/324557, Mosi-o-Tunya Rd
Email: suninzam@zamnet.zm
Web: www.suninternational.com
The five-star Royal Livingstone, operated by Sun International, is part of the Sun complex just a short walk from the Falls. Spectacular views of the Falls from the sundeck on the Zambezi embankment, old-style colonial decor, fine garden, salt water swimming pool.
Voted one of the leading hotels of the world. Check for 'Sun Specials' with the travel agencies.

TAITA FALCON LODGE

Batoka Gorge-Mukuni area
Tel: +260 (03) 321850
Fax: +260 (03) 321850
E-mail: taita-falcon@zamnet.zm

Spectacular view over the gorge, camping facilities & full board available

Taita Falcon Lodge
Tel (03) 321850 /(
263) 11 208387 / 230667,
Fax (03) 321850
Email: taita-falcon@zamnet.zm
Web: www.taitafalcon.com
This lodge is perched above rapid 17 on the very edge of the Batoka Gorge in Makuni area, offering superb views of the raging water 200 meters below. It has ensuite reed chalets, shaded by native bush & open to the gentle winds that blow through the gorge.

Stanley Safari Lodge
Tel (097) 848615/+32-496-67-20-40/
(263) 91 262042, Fax (+)1-206-350-259
Email: info@stanleysafaris.com
Web: www.stanelysafaris.com
Located on Makuni road bordering the Mosi-o-Tunya National Park, this lodge has a feel of 1920s Africa offering thatched cottages with fabulous views of the Falls spray.

Tongabezi
Tel (03) 324450-68/ 095 795260
Fax (03) 324483
Email: tonga@zamnet.zm
Web: www.tongabezi.com
Much-talked about, Tongabezi is one of several places perched along the Zambezi river but far enough apart to retain exclusivity and tranquillity. Tongabezi is made up of luxurious cottages and houses, with spacious rooms & private lounges. The views are made in heaven.

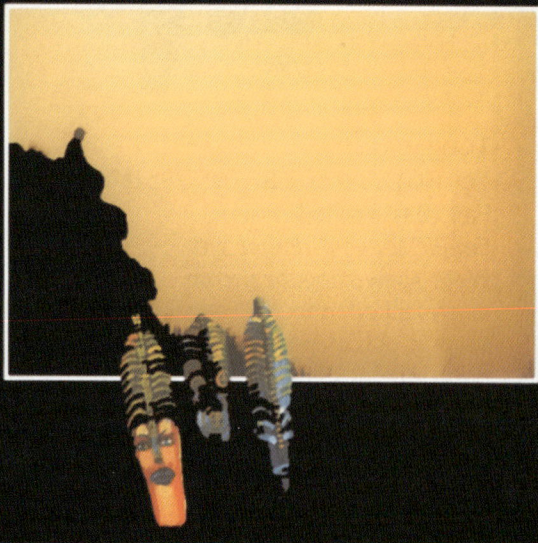

The Zambezi Sun

Tel (03) 321122/322741
Fax (03) 321128, Mosi-o-Tunya Rd
Email: suninzam@zamnet.zm
Web: www.suninternational.com
Sister three-star hotel to the Royal Livingstone and also a great and very comfortable hotel, with a superb location right on the edge of the Eastern Cateract of the Falls. The decor is traditional African colours and designs. A hive of activity, it is ideal for families and has a 'Happy Hippo' club for children.

Chundukwa Lodge

Tel (03) 324452, Fax (03) 324452
Email: chundukwa@zamnet.zm
Web: www.zambiatourism.com/chunduk-wa
Situated 30km upstream from the Falls,this lodge has unique tree houses built on stilts overlooking the Zambezi River. Specialises in horse-riding treks.

The Island of Siankaba

Tel (03) 324490 / 097 720530 / 791241
Email: siankaba@zamnet.zm
Web: www.siankaba.com
Forty km upstream from the Falls and 40 km from the Chobe National Game Park in Botswana boasts of luxurious teak and canvas chalets nestled in a canopy of trees connected by raised walkways, each with own private view of the river.

Renowed for its uniqueness, this special lodge radiates the warmth of its people and offers you understated luxury in a tranquil Zambian atmosphere.

Reservations
+260 3 323235
Lodge: + 260 3 324450 / 68
Email: tonga@zamnet.zm

Private Bag 31
Livingstone
Zambia

THE VICTORIA FALLS ZAMBIA

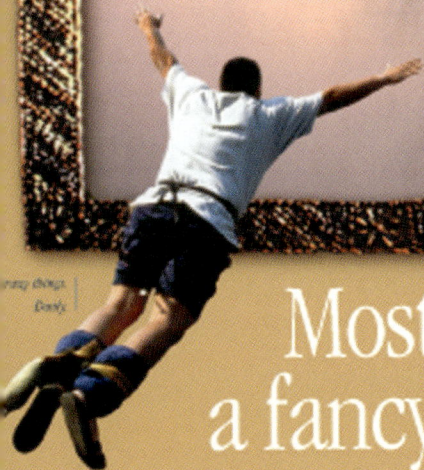

Most hotels have a fancy water feature.

Ours just happens to be one of the world's seven wonders.

I t's the most essential destination in all Africa, one of the world's seven wonders, and also its mightiest waterfall. And now there's a new hotel on the Great Zambezi River to ignite your spirit of adventure.

From the moment you arrive at The Zambezi Sun, you'll be at the heart of The Victoria Falls. In fact, you won't find a place that'll keep you closer to the action. Go on a nature safari – by air, water, land or even by elephant. Or try a day's white water rafting, river boarding, abseiling or bungee jumping. And after a morning's escapades in the bundus, you'll return to the cool waters of a landscaped pool, where you can sip on an exotic cocktail or feast on a buffet lunch.

The Zambezi Sun captures the soul of Africa. It's fun, rustic and relaxing. And it has all of the many activities and facilities that you've come to expect from a Sun International resort.

So the world's essential destination just became a little more essential.

ZAMBEZI SUN
VICTORIA FALLS ZAMBIA

STANLEY SAFARI LODGE

Bordering the Mosi-Oa-Tunya National Park, the exclusive
Stanley Safari Lodge will take you back to the Africa of the 1920's...

Each of the 8 individual thatched cottages are tastefully decorated
and have fabulous en-suite bathrooms with amazing views.

Your stay at Stanely Safari Lodge can be entirely tailor-made.
We offer game drives, safaris in Kafue National Park and
Botswana's Chobe National Park, canoeing, cultural visits...

Fax: +1 206 350 025
Tel: +260 97 848 61
+ 32 496 67204
P.O. Box 604399, the Victoria Fall
Livingstone, Zambi

email: info@stanleysafaris.com   website: www.Stanleysafaris.com

The River Club
Tel (03) 324457/
097 771032 (263) 11 406 563
Email: riverclb@wilderness.co.zw
Web: www.riverclubzam.com
Located off Nakatindi road overlooking the
Zambezi river with open fronted thatched
ensuite chalets including two honeymoon
suites.
Old colonial style setting and very comfortable with pleasant settings. The swimming pool has a magnificent view over the
river for those who wish to relax in the
sun.

Zambezi Royal Chundu Lodge
Tel (03) 321772 /(27) 83 967 1840 /
(27) 11 463 4611
Email: mail@royalchundu.com;
kim@royalchundu.com
Web: www.royalchundu.com
Located about 60 km out of Livingstone,
off Nakatindi road in the same grounds as
Tree-Tops. With chalets set in gardens
overlooking the river, set amid the beautiful Katambora Forest, offers fishing pack-
ages including boat hire and canoe trips.

Songwe Point Village
Farm No 9239, Songwe Village,
Tel (03) 323659/(263) 11 23 1383,
Fax (03) 323659
Email: songwe@zamnet.zm
Web: www.kwando.co.za
Overlooking the gorge and surrounded by
vast areas of protected land offers an
opportunity to embark on a unique cultur-
al adventure in a local Zambian village.
Songwe Museum is within walking distance
or can be visited by traditional ox-cart.

Sussi & Chuma
Tel (263) 9 471225 / 471714-5
Email: info@starofafrica.co.zw
Set in the Mosi-o-Tunya National Park, this
newly opened lodge has spacious architec-
turally designed tree houses. Has comfortable lodging overlooking a beautiful surrounding and makes you feel close to
nature.

Zambezi Water Front Lodge

Tel (03) 320606-7 /320609, Fax (03) 320609   Email:waterfront@zamnet.zm
Lodge that offers a wide range of accommodation to suit all budgets. Has good atmosphere around bar and pool area. Starting point for SafPar activities. Excellent viewing of elephants crossing the Zambezi river.

Middle Range

Lost Horizons Guest Lodge, Tel (097) 859515/ 263 11 212649,
Fax (267) 663 685
Email: reservations@bushways.co.za
Situated a few km from the Falls, this lodge has spectacular views of the mighty Zambezi river. It has comfortable chalets, plus a charming dining & bar area.

Ngolide Lodge

Ngolide Lodge, 110 Mosi-o-Tunya Rd, Tel (03) 321091-2, Fax (03) 321113
Email: ngolide@zamnet.zm
Web: www.zambiatourism.com/ngolide
Thatched lodge situated in the heart of Livingstone, ensuite accommodation, satellite TV, lounge and secure parking.

Nyala LODGE

Nyala Lodge, Tel (03) 322446/ (263) 11 211094, Fax (03) 321248
Email: nyala@zamnet.zm
7km from the Falls on Sichanga road, with thatched chalets bordering the Mosi-oa-Tunya National Park. Offers quiet relaxing atmosphere and a swimming pool.

Kambezi Royal Chundu Safari Lodge / TREETOPS

Tree-Tops Lodge
Tel (03) 321772 /(27) 83 967 1840 / (27) 11 463 4611
Email: mail@tree-tops.com
Web: www.tree-tops.com
60km from Livingstone near the Kasungula pontoon. Built on raised stilts, metres above the Zambezi, under an enormous canopy of waterberry trees.

Natural Mystic, Tel (03) 322812, Fax (03) 322812, Nakatindi Rd
Email: nmlodge@zamnet.zm
Located 20km out of Livingstone on Nakatindi road, with en-suite chalets, bar, restaurant, swimming pool and gift shop.

New Fairmount Hotel & Casino

Tel (03) 320723-8, Fax (03) 321490
Email: nfhc@zamnet.zm
Web: www.fairmount.co.zm
Old colonial three-star hotel located in the centre of town Offers a large swimming pool, casino and nightclub.

Roysam Lodge & Tours Limited

Tel (03) 321072, Fax (03) 321073, Plot 161 Airport Rd
Email: roysam@zamnet.zm
Located enroute to the airport, offers ensuite rooms, air-conditioned with DSTV.

ThornTree River Lodge

Tel (03) 324480,
Fax (03) 324081, Kasangula Rd
Email: thorntree@safpar.co.zw
11 km from Livingstone on the Zambezi river off Nakatindi road with comfortable lodging and basic amenities.

The Wane Guest Lodge
Tel (03) 324058
Cell: 097 749809
Email: wasingo@zamtel.zm
Stand No. 2644/70 Ellen Brittel,
Located as you enter Livingstone from the north (Lusaka). The lodge offers self-contained rooms with satellite TV, fridge and telephone. Transport to Victoria Falls can be arranged upon request. Bookings for activities can be made through the lodge.

Wasawange Lodge
Airport Road,
Tel (03) 324066/ 324141
Fax (03) 324067
Email: waslodge@zamnet.zm
Web: www.tourvicfalls.com
Located 2km from the airport and about 8km away from the Falls. This lodge is a blend of unique African air-conditioned thatched chalets and more conventional rooms and chalets with telephone and TV.

Ngolide Lodge

An exclusive thatched Lodge situated in the heart of Livingstone with a truly ethnic feel. All rooms are en-suite offering satellite TVs, mosquito nets, and Tea / Coffee making facility. We have a fully licenced bar, a restaurant specialising in Indian Cuisine, Lounge and secure parking. All activities can be arranged in the Victoria Falls area.

Tel: +260 3 321091/2
Fax: +260 3 321113
ngolide@zamnet.zm
www.zambiatourism.com/ngolide

MARAMBA RIVER LODGE

Just 4km from the Mighty Victoria Falls

- Ensuite Chalets
- Tents under thatch
- Camping facilities
- Bar and Restaurant
- Swimming Pool
- On site security

Booking office for all adventure activities:
Tel/Fax (260) 3 324189 P.O Box 60957
Livingstone Zambia
Email: maramba@zamnet.zm
Website: www.zambiatourism.com/maramba
www.maramba-zambia.com

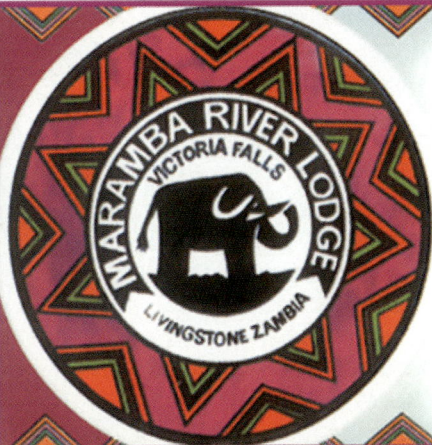

Mo Business Bureau
Heritage House

WE PROVIDE INTERNET & SECRETARIAL SERVICES

Tel: +260 3 320775 Fax: +260 3 320439
P.O. Box 60643, Mosi-o-Tunya Road, Livingstone
email:africanvillage@zamnet.zm

Budget

CHANTERS
GUEST LODGE & RESTAURANT

Chanters Guest Lodge, Tel (03) 323412
Lukulu Crescent, Off Obote Avenue
Sign posted as you enter Livingstone from Lusaka. Guest house and restaurant.

Maramba River Lodge
Tel (03) 324189,
Fax (03) 323130
Email:maramba@zamnet.zm
Web:www.maramba-zambia.com
4km from the Victoria Falls. Set on the banks of the Maramba River in the Mosi-o-Tunya National Park. Shady lawned campsite and budget accommodation with ensuite thatched chalets available.

NAMEL'S
Guest Lodge

Namel's Guest Lodge
Tel (03) 324274/097-772318,
Fax (03) 324274
Email: namel@zamnet.zm.
Located as you enter Livingstone from the north (Lusaka), offers ensuite rooms with all the basic amenities, full English breakfast included.

Papagayo Guest House
Tel (03)320237/263-11-212 587
Email: papagayo@zamnet.zm
Backpackers accommodation in a converted house with private rooms and camping facilities. Laundry, swimming pool, bar, and multi-lingual staff.

Zambezi Ultima Guest House
Tel (03) 320173 / 323534 / 097 752964
Fax (03) 320173, No 36 Likute Way.
Email: ultima@zamnet.zm
Self contained double & single rooms with DSTV Satellite.

Bovu Island
Telefax (03) 323708
Email: jungle@zamnet.zm
Web: www.junglejunction.net
On the Upper Zambezi, offers secluded campsite and camping gear for hire.

Busiku Guest House,
Tel (03) 322468
Email: bod@zamnet.zm
Popular with local cross border business travellers near Maramba township after the Central Police Station.

Fawlty Towers International Backpackers,
Tel (03) 323432,
Fax (03) 323432
Email: ahorizon@zamnet.zm
Web: www.adventure-africa.com
Located in the centre of town, lively backpackers with range of accommodation from dorms to ensuite chalets and camping facilities. With pool, kitchen, bar, very relaxed, great source of information, able to arrange various trips and activities.

Paradise Island
Tel (03) 324227/324214, Fax (03) 324094
Email: bwaato@zamnet.zm
Island 45 km upstream from the falls.

The Grotto Campsite (Grubby's)
Tel (03) 323929/ (263) 11 213731/ 411260, Fax (03) 322370
2 Maambo Way
Walking distance from the centre of town offering basic accommodation.
Ideal for budget travellers, camping available.

Jollyboys International Backpackers,
Tel (03) 324229, Fax (03) 324229
Email: jollybs@zamnet.zm
www:backpackzambia.com
Located on 34 Kanyanta road, very popular with good facilities including bar, kitchen and Internet. Offers camping facilities. Great source of information, free lifts to the Falls, can arrange all sorts of trips and activities.

Gecko's, Tel (03) 322267,
Fax (03) 322267
Email: gecko@zamnet.zm
Limulunga Road,
Friendly and clean accommodation with shared bathrooms. Fully-equipped self-catering kitchen, garden and swimming pool.

Jungle Junction
Telefax (03) 323708
Email: jungle@zamnet.zm
Web: www.junglejunction.net
Stay in a jungle hut on a palm fringed tropical Island, 50 kms upstream at Katombora Rapids, sling a hammock and chill out on a lush island.

The Mission Backpackers
Tel (03) 323084
Email: missionbackpackers@hotmail.com
Located in the centre of town, good place for budget travellers. Clean, secure and central.

Libala Inn
Tel (03) 322683/097 823632
Fax (03) 322122
Email: etthompson@zamnet.zm
32 Katete Road
Simple setting further away from the Falls.

Mutemwa Camp, Tel +(27) 11 8882431,
Fax +(27) 11 8885798
Email: zambezi@mweb.co.za.
Campsite.

FEGO
Caffé

Fego Café, Tel (03) 321122/322362
Email: tub2000@hotmail.com
Located at the Falls Activity Centre.
Coffee Shop, Sun International

Funky Munky

Funky Munky
Tel (03) 320120,Fax (03) 323455,
Plot 214, Mosi-o-Tunya Rd.
Pizza Bistro, Classic pizzas cooked in a traditional stone oven, spicy pittas & schawarmas, all day breakfasts, salads, sandwiches & rolls. Cheap & cheerful! Eat in or take away.

African Skies, Tel (03) 324189
Located at Maramba Lodge, see, feel and taste the flavours of Africa. Serves breakfast, brunch, lunch and dinner.

Hippo's
Tel (03) 322696,
Fax (03) 323432,
Email: ahorizon@zamnet.zm
Located at the back of Fawlty Towers, set in a delightful garden, restaurant and bar offering a variety of meals at good value.

Hungry Lion, Mosi-o-Tunya Road
Take away.

Laughing Dragon, Tel 097 846919,
Located behind the Postoffice off Mosi-o-Tunya Road.
Chinese cuisine.

Mukamba (Ann's Steak House)
Tel (03) 324424
Opposite the Angilcan Church, specialises in German and Zambian foods.

Ngolide Lodge Restaurant
Tel (03) 321091-2, Fax (03) 321113
Located on Mosi-o-Tunya Road within the lodge, serves Indian cuisine.

Ocean Basket
Tel (03) 321288/263-11-603401,
Fax (03) 324236
825 Mosi-o-Tunya Road
South African chain, fish speciality restaurant.

The Mission Bar & Restaurant
Tel (03) 323084
Located on Mosi-o-Tunya.

Pub and Grill (Rite Investments)
Tel (03) 320398/097 796708
Plot 3097/98, Mosi-o-Tunya Road.

Utsav
Tel (03) 322259/03 323333
Fax (03) 323333, Plot 357
Mosi-o-Tunya Rd,
Email: utsav@zamnet.zm
Indian cuisine at prices for all pockets.

Zigzag Café
Tel (03) 322814/324081
Mosi-o-Tunya Road
Coffee, snacks and cakes, best place for cappuccinos, milkshakes and smoothies.

ADVENTURE SPECIALISTS

Across Africa
Tel (03) 320823,
Fax (03) 320277
Email: aaover@zamnet.zm
Tailor-made hunting safaris.

African Queen
Tel (03) 321513 / (263) 11 417 953, Fax
(03) 324070
*Email:african.queen@thevictoriafalls.
co.zm,*
Web: www.theafricanqueen.co.za
Offers luxury boat cruises on the Zambezi.

Angle Zambia, Tel (03) 324489,
Fax +263 (11) 212251
Email: angle@zamnet.zm
Fishing excursions on the Zambezi.

Batoka Skies, Tel (03) 320058/263 11
409 578, Fax (03) 324071
Email: freedom@zamnet.zm
Offers microlighting and helicopter rides.

Bundu Adventures, Tel (03) 324407,
Fax (03) 324406
Email: zambezi@zamnet.zm
Web: www.bundu-adventures.com
Offers rafting on the Zambezi river.

Bwaato Adventures, Tel (03) 324227
/321830 /097 712249-50,
Fax (03) 324227
Email: bwaato@zamnet.zm
Variety of activities on the Zambezi river.

The Falls Resort, Tel (03) 321122,
Fax (03) 321128
Email: suninzam@zamnet.zm
One-stop activity centre for reservations.

Jet Extreme, Tel (03) 323929 /324024,
Fax (03) 322370
Email: jetextreme@zamnet.zm
Web: www.raftextreme.com
Jet boating in the gorge, whitewater rafting, riverboarding & tandem kayaking.

Serious Fun, Telefax (03) 322128
Email: seriousfun@zamnet.zm
Offers surfing on the Zambezi.

Touch Adventure, Telefax (03) 323095
Email: raft@touchadventure.com
Offering tours and adventure.

United Air Charter, Tel (03) 323095
/263 11 407 573, Fax (03) 323095
Email: uac@zamnet.zm
Web: www.uaczam.com
Offers helicopter trips over the Victora
Falls and other activities.

Victoria Falls River Safaris
Tel (03) 323587 / 095 436119,
Fax (03) 323587
Email: riversafaris@zamnet.zm
Web: www.vicfallriversafaris.com
Offers various safari tour options.

The Zambezi Adventure Centre
Tel (03) 326629
Email: safpar@zamnet.zm
Offers white water rafting, riverboarding,
tandem kayaking, jetboating, elephant
back safari, horse trails, abseiling, gorge
swing and bungee jumping.

Zambezi Booze Cruise
Tel (03) 324081
Email: taonga@zamnet.zm
Near the Boat Club, for fun Zambezi river
cruises.

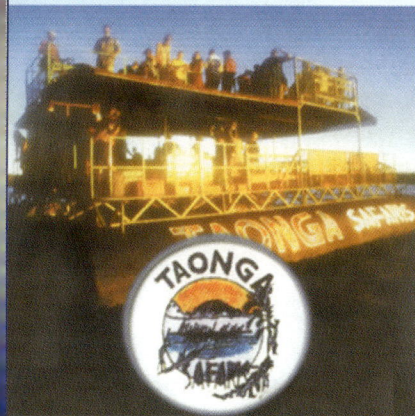

SOUTHEND BUREAU-DE-CHANGE

Southend Bureau de Change
Liso House, 106 Mosi-o-Tunya Rd,
Tel (03) 320241 /320773,
Fax (03) 322128
Email: southend@zamnet.zm
Bureau de Change.

Zulunet Internet Café & Gallery

Compu-art Design Pty (Zulunet)
116c Mosi-o-Tunya Road,
Tel (03) 322985, Fax (03) 322985
Email: zulunet@zamnet.zm
Website: www.zulunet.fws1.com
Internet Café & Arts & Crafts.

CYBER POST — INTERNET CAFE —

Cyber Post, 216 Mosi-o-Tunya Road,
Tel (03) 321338, Fax (03) 321338
Email: cyberpost@zamnet.zm
Internet Café.

Health Point (Z) Ltd. Medical Centre

Health Point (Z) Ltd, Tel (03) 322170
/097-794888, Fax (03) 322922,2644/401
Mushili Way
Email: shanks@zamnet.zm
Medical Centre.

KENWOOD power in COMMUNICATION

Kenwood, Cell (097) 772744
Email: fdxliv@zamnet.zm
Communication.

KONICA PHOTO EXPRESS

Konica-Photo Express
117 Mosi-o-Tunya Road,
Tel (03) 323322, Fax (03) 323332
Email: stiku@zamnet.zm
Photography.

KUBU CRAFTS

Kubu Crafts, Tel (03) 324093 / 321669
/263 11 208946, Fax (03) 324093
Email: kubucrafts@zamnet.zm
Website: www.kubucrafts.com
133 Mosi-o-Tunya Road.
African furniture shop & crafts.

Mo Money Bureau de Change Ltd
Licensed Foreign Currency Dealers
Stanley House - Livingstone

Mo Money Bureau de Change
Tel (03) 323431, Fax (03) 324474
Ground Floor, Stanley House, Mosi-o-
Tunya Rd,
Email: momoney@zamnet.zm
Bureau de Change.

Tel (01) 237933, (01) 237933
Fairview Hotel, Church Road,
Email: momoney@pop3.zamtel.zm
Bureau de Change.

Mo Business Bureau
Tel (03) 320775, Fax (03) 320439
Heritage House, Mosi-o-Tunya Road,
Email: africanvillage@zamnet.zm
Business Centre.

On the way to Livingstone

The journey from Lusaka to Livingstone will take you through a number of small towns where you can stock up on fuel and other provisions, including Mazabuka, the heart of the farming district which boasts Zambia's only hypermarket, and Monze.

The only place really worth stopping off, especially if you are interested in culture, is the small town of Choma.

The excellent Choma Museum(Tel 032 20394) is located in an old colonial school dating from the 1920s which is one of the oldest preserved buildings in Zambia. The exhibits are mainly of the local Tonga people, there's a contemporary art exhibition and well-stocked crafts shops, with great baskets at good prices. The three huge metal balls in the garden were strung on battleship chains and pulled by bulldozers to clear the vegetation in preparation for the massive Kariba Dam.

LOCHINVAR NATIONAL PARK

This small park, which lies south of the Kafue River as shown in the map on the next page, is slowly being rehabilitated after years of neglect and rampant poaching.

The park has been designated by the World Wide Fund for Nature as a 'wetland of international importance' and the WWF is working with the local people to manage the park on a sustainable basis for the people and animals.

Lochinvar's main feature is the Chunga Lagoon, a paradise for birdwatchers. More than 400 species of birds have been recorded in Lochinvar, which from 1913 to 1965 was a cattle ranch. Other attractions are the Iron Age settlement at Sebanzi Hill and Gwisho Hot Springs, which are surrounded by fan palms.

The springs occur because of a geological fault, which also creates the mineral gypsum, used to make plaster of paris and mined here in the 1970s.

To get to Lochinvar, drive from Lusaka to Monze on the Livingstone road. The park is about 48km from Monze.

In Monze take the road signposted to Namwala, which passes through Chongo and forks about 8km afterwards.

Take the right fork, then after about 10km turn left at a sign and follow the road.

The Star of Africa group has rehabilitated the park's accommodation, transforming Lochinvar House, the farmhouse of the original owner of Lochinvar estate into a pleasant, small lodge aimed at

self-drive visitors and creating Lechwe Plains Tented Camp, which consists of luxury canvas pavilions placed on teak decking near the water's edge.

Tel: +(263) 9 471225/471715/471837, email: *info@starofafrica.co.zw and reservations@starofafrica.co.zw*, web: *www.starofafrica.com*

PLACES TO STAY

Gwembe Safari Lodge
Tel (032) 20169/20021/20119,
Fax (032) 20054,
Cell (097) 803292 /777719,
Email: gwemsaf@coppernet.zm,
Web: www.gwemsafaris.com
Located 2km south of Choma, family run lodge, with thatched chalets and ensuite facilities. Offers camping facilities, swimming pool, tennis & volleyball courts.

The Moorings Campsite, Tel (032) 50049 / 097 863241
Email: tsavory@zamnet.zm
Located outside Monze, is a very well laid out campsite, ideal place to break your journey.

Lake View Lodge, Tel (032) 20169 /20021 /20119, Fax (032) 20054 / 20570, Cell (097) 803292 / 777719,
Email:gwemsaf@zamnet.zm; gwemsaf@coppernet.zm,
Located in Sinazongwe on Lake Kariba about midway between Lusaka and Livingstone. Offers thatched self contained chalets.

40 Winks Guest House
Tel (097) 884767/(032) 30340-1
Email: dcclayton@zamnet.zm
Located in Mazabuka.

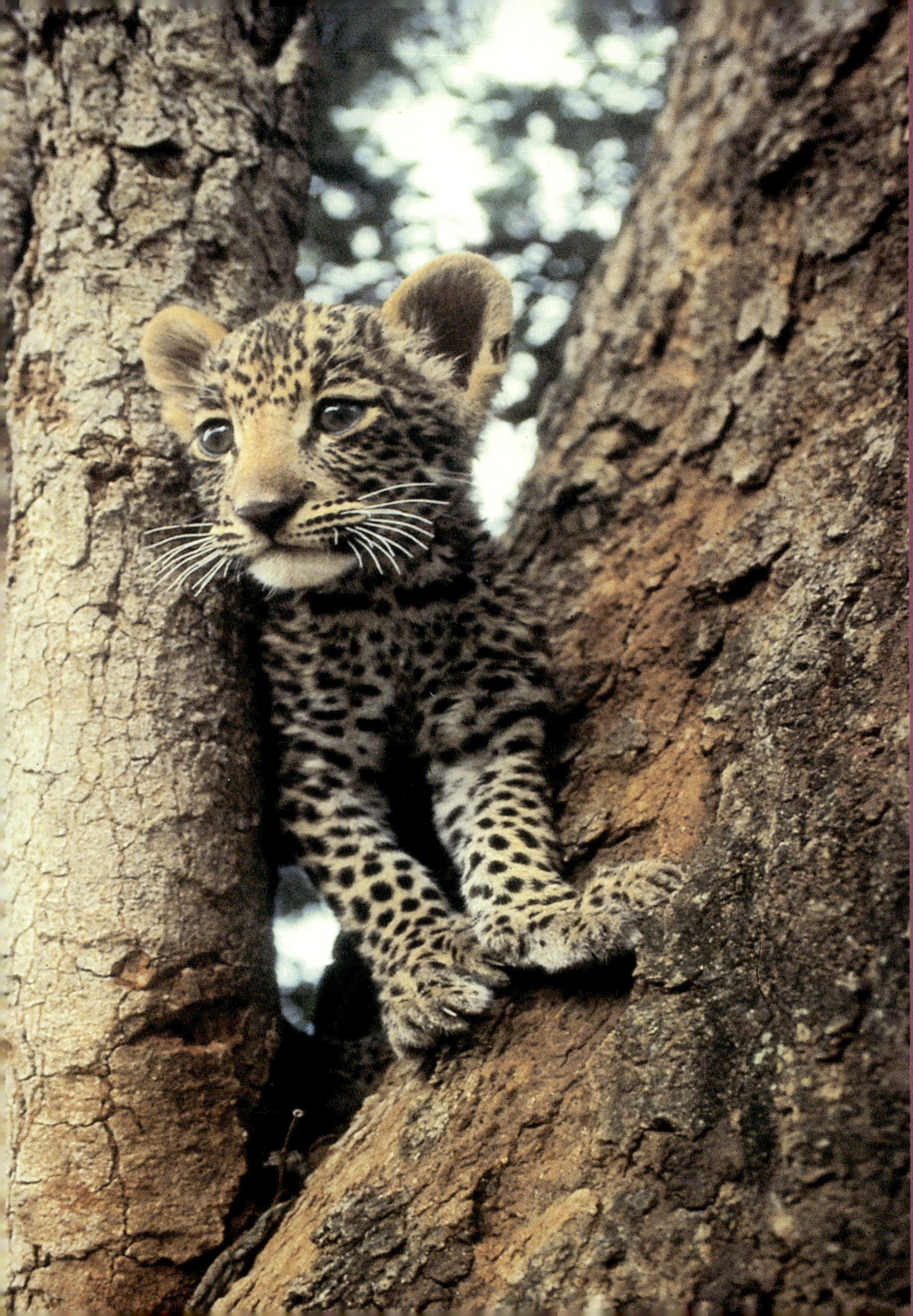

LUANGWA VALLEY

Most visitors to Zambia, especially first-timers, head east to Luangwa Valley, an offshoot of the Great Rift Valley which cuts through Eastern and Southern Africa, which is home to two gems of national parks.

If you're after a true African safari experience then either North or South Luangwa National Park will give you just that, rewarding you with an experience that is hard to beat.

Not as well known as South Luangwa, North Luangwa's greatest charm is the fact that it is a completely unspoiled and remote African wilderness. The park is 4,636 sq km in size, lies on the western side of the mighty Luangwa River, upstream of the south Luangwa National Park. At its heart is the lovely Mwaleshi river, a tributary of the Luangwa River, dotted along which are a number of specialized camps and lodges, which are open only during the dry May to November season.

Visitors sometimes combine a trip here with Northern Zambia, including Kasanka National Park and the incongruous English manor house set in the African bush known as Shiwa N'gandu (see page 211).

South Luangwa is the better known and more accessible of the two parks, offering a large choice of top-class accommodation, breath-taking scenery and a wide variety of animals. Many visitors are drawn to 'the Valley', as it's known locally, year after year, each time experiencing something different and special. Sprawling over 9000 sq km and home to about 100 mammal species and 400 bird species, this stunning national park lies between the meandering Luangwa River and the imposing Muchinga Escarpment. Its reputation as Zambia's best and one of the most outstanding parks Africa has to offer is well deserved - you won't be disappointed.

Some of the best guides in Zambia enrich the Valley experience. They strive to maintain the Valley's reputation as one of the more progressive

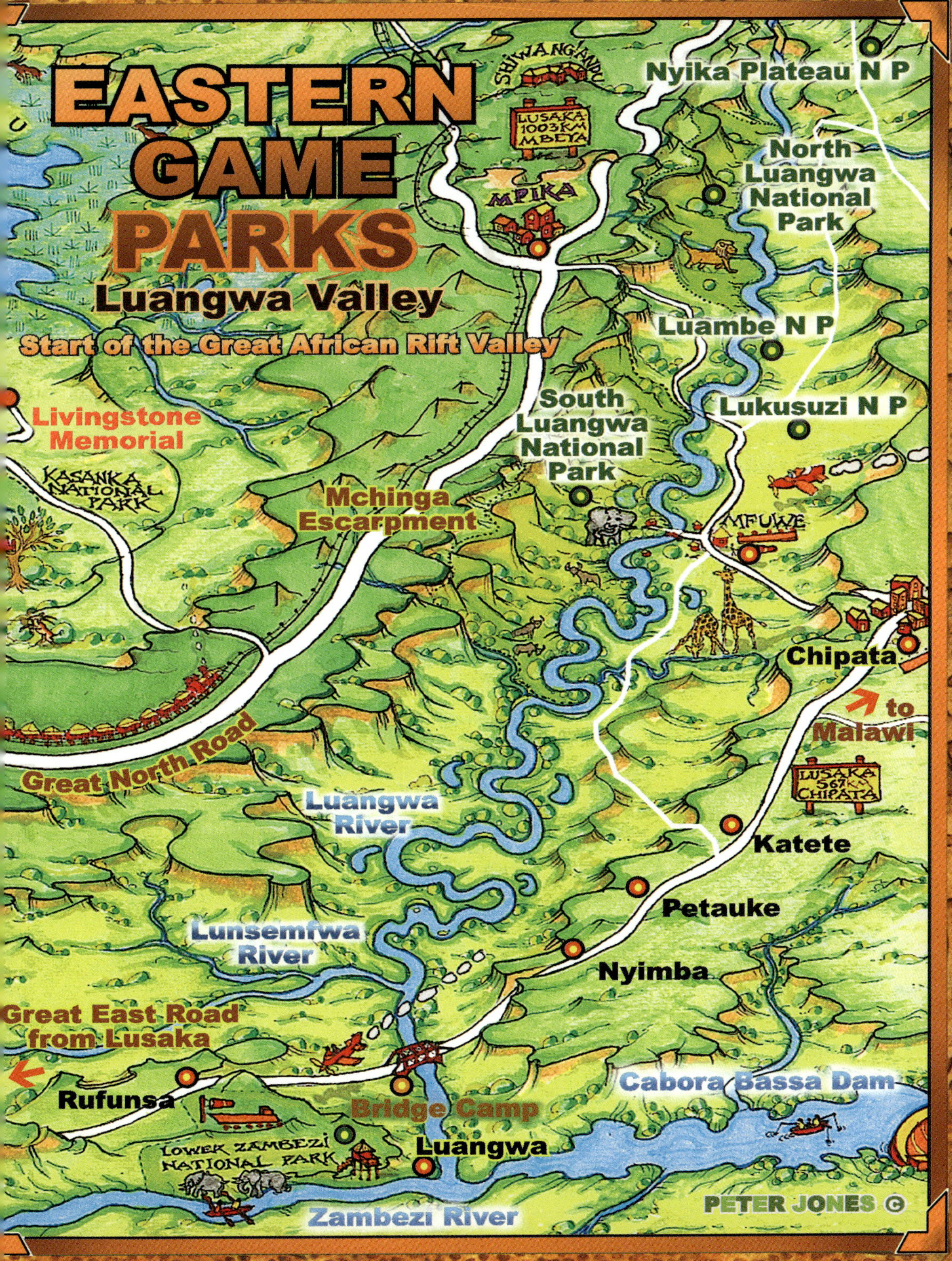

EASTERN GAME PARKS
Luangwa Valley
Start of the Great African Rift Valley

SHIWANGANDU

LUSAKA 1003KM MBEYA

MPIKA

Nyika Plateau N P

North Luangwa National Park

Luambe N P

Lukusuzi N P

Livingstone Memorial

KASANKA NATIONAL PARK

Mchinga Escarpment

South Luangwa National Park

MFUWE

Chipata

to Malawi

LUSAKA 567KM CHIPATA

Great North Road

Luangwa River

Katete

Petauke

Lunsemfwa River

Nyimba

Great East Road from Lusaka

Rufunsa

Cabora Bassa Dam

Bridge Camp

Luangwa

LOWER ZAMBEZI NATIONAL PARK

Zambezi River

PETER JONES ©

national parks in Zambia. After being put through vigorous tests, most are a fount of information about the habits of animals, birds and the properties of the park's vegetation.

South Luangwa is the birthplace of people-based conservation and the walking safari, thanks to the influential and visionary Norman Carr. One of the park's first rangers, in 1950 Carr opened up some of the tribal land belonging to Chief Nsefu (the eastern part of the park now known as the Nsefu area) to the public. The entrance fees went directly to the local community, one of the first community conservation schemes in Africa years ahead of its time.

A decade later, Carr pioneered the walking safari, an exhilarating way of not just getting close to the big and small animals but also of becoming part of the African bush, an often-overlooked experience.

At the heart of South Luangwa is the

NORMAN CARR

Mfuwe area. Several lodges and camps are clustered close to the main entrance to the park, the Mfuwe bridge over the Luangwa River, and nearby is Mfuwe village (now more like a town after an influx in recent years of urbanisation), which has shops, bars, a market and a petrol station.

The area of the national park west of the Mfuwe main entrance is a popular and rewarding place for game viewing. You are unlikely to meet too many other vehicles during a game drive in South Luangwa, but traffic is growing in the Mfuwe area.

If you want total quiet, exclusivity and are prepared for a longer drive or transfer from the airport, then try the lodges and camps in the more remote northern and southern parts of the park where there are fewer visitors.

Much of the park is closed during the rainy season or the so-called 'green season' (December to April) when smaller tracks become impassable and the Luangwa river rises by several metres.

The wide Luangwa River is the lifeblood of the park, but unlike in other Zambian parks, trips by boat and canoe are not a major feature in South Luangwa. When the Luangwa is in full flow, chunks of trees often get swept downstream and boating can be very dangerous. In the dry season, it becomes so shallow that huge sandbanks are exposed and become covered with basking hippos and crocodiles. The Luangwa's steep banks mean that animals drink at oxbow lakes, glimmering patches of water created as the river changes its course from year to year.

You'll never get bored of Luangwa's landscape, which varies from open grassy plains, with natural salt springs which attract thousands of birds including yellow-billed storks, to strips of woodland alongside the river, sometimes gathered in imposing groves of ebony, mahogany, leadwood and winter thorn trees.

Luangwa's wildlife is glorious (see also National Parks section page 49). Local specialties include Cookson's wildebeest, an unusual, lighter-coloured sub-species, the endemic Thornicroft's giraffe, which has a darker neck pattern than other giraffes, and Crawshay's zebra, which have numerous thin stripes extending down to their hooves and under their belly. The park is a great place to see lions and, on the Luangwa speciality of night drives, the magnificent leopard.

Encouragingly, the numbers of elephants, once nearly wiped out by ivory poachers, are now healthy – but you won't see the big 'tuskers'. For some as yet unknown reason the elephants are much smaller in the Valley than elsewhere in Zambia and indeed Africa.

Another development is the growing population of wild dogs, one of the rarest animals in Zambia and Africa. Sightings of these delightfully sociable animals are a memorable experience.

Bird life highlights include brightly coloured carmine bee-eaters, whose migration here every August to nest in

the sandy river banks is a wonderful sight; quirky queleas, lively Lilian's love-birds, crowned cranes, pelicans and yellow-billed storks which cluster noisily in tall trees in a spectacular colony near Luangwa's salt pans.

Luangwa Valley safaris are spectacular. You can drive yourself but part of the Valley's selling-point is the great care it takes to ensure the safari experience is without a hitch: in almost all cases, all the details are just right and guests are given the holiday of a lifetime.

You'll be really unlucky not to see much game and, if you're booked into one of the top-end lodges, the whole safari experience is reminiscent of days gone by, where all the needs of the guests are anticipated and met. (see National Parks section page 49).

Your visit may coincide with one of the performances given to the lodges by the Malambo Drama Group, set up by one of Norman Carr's granddaughters, Miranda Guhrs, and made up of inspiring and talented local dramatists. The group's most well-known play is the Chipembele: Horn of Sorrow, which explores in a lively and compelling way the demise of Luangwa's black rhino (chipembele) due to the poaching of the 1980s.

Future plans for the group include opening up an outdoor theatre and cultural centre.

Poaching still continues, though not in such a devastating way. To understand how local people are involved in the fight to stamp it out, visit the base of the RATS (Rapid Action Team) in Mfuwe Village.

If you want to meet local people, a visit to Kawaza Village near Mfuwe is recommended. It's not a set-up for tourists, though it is assisted by Robin Pope Safaris, but rather an ecotourism scheme set up by the residents so that visitors can benefit from a real insight into local life and local people can benefit from tourism. Visitors can spend the night in the village's guest hut, eat, drink and socialize the Zambian way. The money goes to social projects such as building a new school.

Chipembele Wildlife Educational Centre, at the confluence of the Chowo and Luangwa Rivers 6km south of Kafunta River Lodge, opened in May 2001 to provide free wildlife and conservation education to local schools. The Centre features a large museum, library and TV video facilities. Tourists are welcome to visit, though please contact them first via your lodge.

Mango Tree Crafts and Tribal Textiles, on the road to the airport, are a couple of the growing number of artists' initiatives that now sell a wide range of distinctive locally produced goods to visitors.

At the airport, which also has money-changing facilities, you can pick up last-minute presents, books, music and cards at Magenge Shop. If you have time to kill before your flight, indulge yourself at the fabulous Moondog Café where you can sip margaritas and munch on enchiladas and other unusual food for the bush. Tel (062) 45068/ 46133

SOUTH LUANGWA
NATIONAL PARK

Muchinga Escarpment

O **Lodges & Camps**
O **Bush Camps**

Chibembe

Big Lagoon

Crocodile Camp

Lion Camp

Tafika

Mwamba

Kaingo

NSEFU SECTOR

Mchenja

Nsefu

Kakuli

Tena Tena

MFUWE AREA

Mfuwe Lodge

MFUWE

TO CHIPATA

Chichele

Flatdogs

Airport

Kapamba River

Kuyenda

Magenge Craft

Chamilandu

Chindeni

Nyamaluma

Bilimungwe

Lusangazi

Luamfwa

Luangwa River

Peter Jones

HOW TO GET THERE

Most people travelling to South Luangwa fly into Mfuwe Airport, about 25 km from Mfuwe village and served by flights most days from Lusaka and Malawi's capital Lilongwe.

Top-end lodges will meet you for free and drive you to the lodge, while budget places usually charge. For drivers, Mfuwe is easily accessible from Chipata (130km). The 560km road journey from Lusaka to Chipata usually takes 7-8 hours and some stretches of road between Nyimba and Chipata are badly potholed.

For Lusakans in search of adventure, there is a rougher back road into South Luangwa via Petauke, which is only passable during the dry season.

But before tackling that route, it's advisable to get an update on road conditions by checking first with tour or lodge operators. Long distance buses

LUANGWA RIVER

operate between Lusaka and Chipata and local minibuses carry passengers between Chipata and Mfuwe.

Chipata is a large, lively town about 20km from Zambia's eastern border with Malawi.

Surrounded by hills, it's worth an overnight stop if you need to stock up on supplies and fuel or fancy a short trip to see some interesting rock art at nearby Thandwe.

The town has a few good value but basic places to stay.

PLACES TO STAY ON ROUTE

Bridge Camp, Tel:(01) 290146, (096) 751302 / 761271, Fax: (01) 295546
Email: rshenton@zamnet.zm
Web: www.zambiantourism.com/changachanga
A great place to break your journey east, just a few kms off the main road before Luangwa Bridge. Chalet and camping facilities available. Access by boat from here to the Lower Zambezi National Park.

Chipata Council Motel
Tel: (062) 21540, Fax: (062) 21540

Crystal Springs Hotel
Tel: (062) 22006/21154/22537, Fax: (062) 22532

Kamocho Guest House
Tel: (062) 22065, Fax: (062) 22065

Katuta Lodge
Tel: 062 21240, Fax: (062) 21240,
Email:mambokb@zamnet.zm

THINGS TO DO ON ROUTE

PLACES TO STAY IN SOUTH LUANGWA

Top Range

Chichele Lodge
Tel:- +263 9 471225/ 471714-5
Fax:- +263 12 45970
Web: www.star_of_africa.com
Email: info@starofafrica.co.zw
Luxury Victorian-style safari lodge on a magnificent hilltop site situated within the South Luangwa Park and overlooking Luangwa River.

Kafunta River Lodge
Tel: (062) 46046,
Web: www.Luangwa.com
Email: kafunta@super-hub.com
This beautiful lodge is set in riverine forest on the banks of the river. with thatched chalets set on stilts overlooking the park. They also operate a superb bush camp that will take you deep into the African wilderness. See details of walking safari bush camps.

Crocodile Camp

Chikwinda Gate

Mwamba River

Lion Camp

Tafika Camp

Mfuwe Road

Luangwa River

Mambwa Bush Camp

Kauluzi Road

Kaingo Camp

Nsefu Camp

Chichele River

Mchenja Camp

NORTH

Kakuli Camp

Kauluzi River

Tena Tena Camp

NSEFU SECTOR

Miliyoti Gate

PETER JONES ©

SOUTH LUANGWA NATIONAL PARK

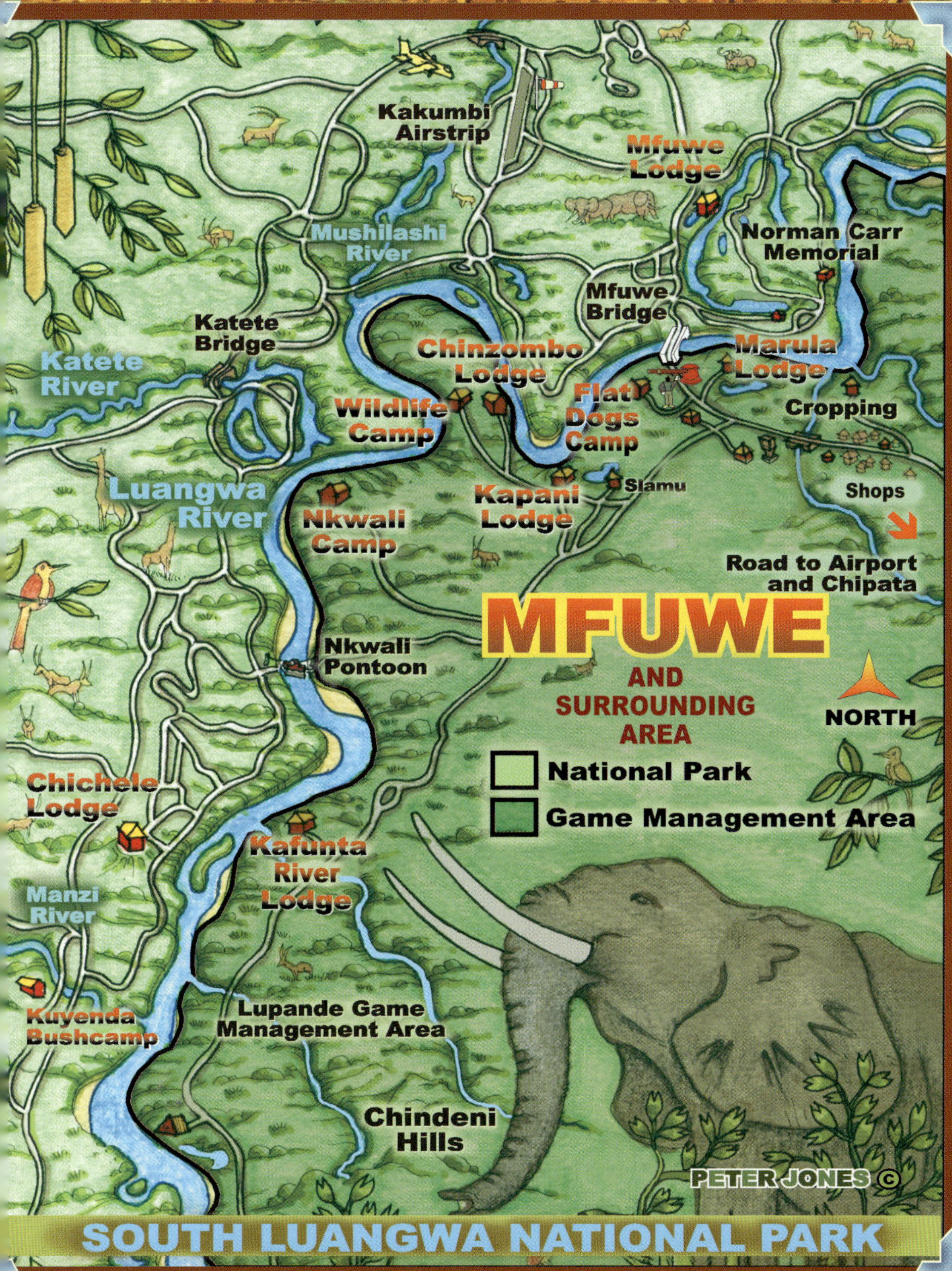

Kakumbi
Airstrip

Mfuwe
Lodge

Norman Carr
Memorial

Mushilashi
River

Mfuwe
Bridge

Katete
Bridge

Chinzombo
Lodge

Marula
Lodge

Katete
River

Wildlife
Camp

Flat
Dogs
Camp

Cropping

Luangwa
River

Nkwali
Camp

Kapani
Lodge

Slamu

Shops

Road to Airport
and Chipata

Nkwali
Pontoon

MFUWE

AND
SURROUNDING
AREA

NORTH

National Park

Game Management Area

Chichele
Lodge

Manzi
River

Kafunta
River
Lodge

Kuyenda
Bushcamp

Lupande Game
Management Area

Chindeni
Hills

PETER JONES ©

SOUTH LUANGWA NATIONAL PARK

Kaingo Camp, Tel: (062) 45064
Web: www.kaingo.com
Email: info@kaingo.com /
2shensaf@bushmail.net
Set in a remote part of the South Luangwa on the bank of the Luangwa river. Also operates a bushcamp. Offers off season river excursions.

Kapani Lodge, Tel: (062) 45015,
Fax: (062) 45025
Web: www.normancarrsafaris.com
Email: kapani@normancarrsafaris.com
Situated on a quiet lagoon beside the Luangwa river, this is pure, old-fashioned luxury in the bush. Norman Carr set up this lodge and the hospitable staff have carried on the tradition of great service, fabulous food and brilliant safaris.

Lion Camp
Email: 2LION@bushmail.net
One of the few camps situated inside the park, it is elevated on stilts along the banks of a lagoon keeping it cool and enhancing the view.

Luamfwa Lodge, Tel: (01) 261683,
(097) 802524, Fax: (01) 262438
Web: www.luamfwa.com
Email: transcat@zamnet.zm
A photographic walking safari camp, overlooking the lagoon.

Mfuwe Lodge, Tel/Fax: (062) 45041,
Satphone: +871 76 228 0123
Web: www.mfuwelodge.com
Email: mfuwe.lodge@super-hub.com
Situated inside the park, this luxury lodge boasts top-class hospitality.

Luangwa River Lodge
Tel: (062) 46032
Email: luangwariverlodge@zamtel.zm
New establishment, located 10 to 15km upstream from the gate. Offers walking safaris and canoeing activities.

Nkwali Lodge, Tel: (062) 45090,
Fax: (062) 49094
Web: www.robinpopesafaris.net
Email: rps@super-hub.com
Located in a most magnificient spot, overlooking the Luangwa and the park.

Tafika Camp, Tel: + 264 61 240561
Web:www.remoteafrica.com
Email: tafika@remoteafrica.com
Located in the north of the park in a remote and stunning bank of the Luangwa. This friendly and comfortable lodge has beautiful surroundings to relax. Uniquely offers canoe safaris and microflights.

WALKING SAFARIS

The Walking Safari Bush Camps

The walking camps are located throughout the South Luangwa National Park situated in the more remote areas of the park. Some safari bush camps are between two and four hours walking apart. A professional guide and an armed game scout accompany each walk.

Seasonal camps are tented or made from local material with thatch and reed twine, the rooms have ensuite facilities with flush toilets. The camps are beautifully sited in the shady wood-

GAME VIEWING SOUTH LUANGWA

land with views either over the Luangwa River or it's tributaries.

The atmosphere in each camp is very different, which adds to the richness of the experience. The bar is open until all guests retire to bed and special dietary requirements are catered for if requested in advance. Activities include picnics, walking, bird watching and game viewing. The time to visit is between 1 June to 31 October before the onset of the rains.

Billimangwe Trails Camp, Chamilandu Bush Camp, Chindeni Trails Camp and Kuyenda Bushcamp operate from Mfuwe lodge and further details can be obtained by contacting them on
Tel/Fax: (062) 45041
Satphone: + 871 76 228 0123
Web:www.bushcampcompany.com
Email: bushcamps@super-hub.com

Norman Carr Safaris, the pioneer of the walking safari, operates a number of bushcamps during the dry season, which include the following:-

Kakuli Bushcamp: This camp accommodates 10 people in spacious safari tents with open air ensuite facilities and overlooks the floodplain at the confluence of the Luwi and Luangwa rivers.

Luwi Bushcamp: Four simple but luxurious thatched bamboo rooms accommodating up to 8 guests, hot showers, flush toilets and solar lights.

Mchenja Bushcamp: This camp sleeps up to 10 people in comfortable thatched huts with ensuite facilities.

Nsolo Camp: 4 thached grass chalets, accommodating up to 8 guests with ensuite facilities. Contact details for the above camps are; Tel: (062) 45015,
Fax: (062) 45025
Web: www.normancarrsafaris.com
Email: kapani@normancarrsafaris.com

Robin Pope Safaris, also one of the leaders in the pack of luxury tented safari camps, operating:

Nsefu Camp, lying in the secluded Nsefu area of the park, has luxurious ensuite chalets.

Tena Tena Camp
Tel: (062) 45090/45051
Fax: (062) 45090
Web: www.robinpopesafaris.net
Email: rps@super-hub.com
Has large comfortable ensuite tents. The camps allow total luxury amidst unbelievable natural settings.

Middle Range

Marula Lodge, Tel: (062) 45073,
Built close to the main Mfuwe entrance near Croc Valley. Basic accomodation, popular with the local Chipata fraternity.

Budget

The Croc Farm, Tel: (062) 45074
Email: mfucroc@super-hub.com
Campsite and chalets built on the banks of the Luangwa River.

Flat Dogs Camp
Tel: (062) 45068/74, 46038
Website: www.flatdogscamp.com
Email: info@flatdogscamp.com
       flatdogscampafrica.com
A unique, friendly camp set on the Luangwa River. Offers a variety of accommodation from campsite to double-storey villas. Popular with overland truck compa-nies. Lively bar popular with locals, restaurant well recomended.

The Wildlife Camp
Tel: (062) 46026/49 , Fax: (062) 45026
Web: www.wildlifecamp-zambia.com
Email: wildlife@super-hub.com
Situated on the banks of the Luangwa River, this camp has a variety of accommodation from campsites and self-catering to fully catered chalets. The camp is located outside the Park.

PLACES TO STAY IN NORTH LUANGWA

The handful of camps in North Luangwa National Park are dotted along the Mwaleshi River and cater mainly for all-inclusive visitors. They are open only in the dry season (May-November).

There are very few roads in North Luangwa and the emphasis is very much on walking safaris. Sensible 4WD drivers can reach North Luangwa via the Great North Road (coming from Lusaka, turn off right 55 km north of Mpika and follow the steep road down the Muchinga Escarpment into the park).

It is also possible to drive the 230km route from South Luangwa to North Luangwa but be prepared for a long day's drive and some wading through rivers.

Independent travellers should always book accommodation in advance, obtain an update on road conditions and routes. GPS co-ordinates are an advantage.

Top range

Buffalo Camp
Email: reservations@zamsaf.com
The camp is situated on the banks of the Mwaleshi River. Specializes in walking safaris. Bookings can also be arranged through Kapishya Lodge (Shiwa Ngandu) or Kasanka National Park.

Kutandula Camp, *Web: kutandula.com*
Email: kuta@francetelecom.fr

Mwaleshi Camp
Website:www.remoteafrica.com
Email: info@remoteafrica.com
Ensuite walking bush camp on the Mwaleshi river. Magnificent view from the camp. Own airstrip. Guests take a 30-minute flight from Tafika camp.

WALKING SAFARIS

BLACK SABLE

KAFUE AND THE WEST

The mighty Zambezi River is central to the history and way of life in Zambia's remote, wild and beautiful Western Province. The most dramatic manifestation of this imposing river is one of Zambia's most colourful and intriguing cultural ceremonies, the Kuomboka ceremony (see the section on Traditional Ceremonies, page 33).

Kuomboka, which means to get out of water, is celebrated by the Lozi people in a part of Western Province known as Barotseland to mark the movement of their traditional ruler, the Litunga, from his palace on the Zambezi flood plain to his palace on higher ground. It's Zambia's best-known ceremony and worth the long trip out west. The region is also the site of another journey: the breathtaking spectacle of Africa's second largest wildebeest migration into the remote and rarely visited Liuwa Plains National Park.

More well-known is the vast Kafue National Park, slowly regaining its former status as one of Zambia's best game-viewing areas, and also dominated by a grand river. The huge Kafue River, which starts in the Copperbelt, flows through the heart of the park. Beyond the park, the river flows through a great flood plain known as the Kafue Flats, part of which is protected by two small national parks, Lochinvar and the Blue Lagoon.

KAFUE NATIONAL PARK

Covering over 22,000 sq km of bush, the Kafue National Park is two and a half times bigger than South Luangwa.

Officially, the park is open all year, but most of the camps and lodges are not open during the height of the rainy season and, for everything but the birds, the best time to visit is in the dry season, i.e. 1 June to 15 November. Of all Zambian parks, Kafue National Park probably has the greatest diversity of mammal species, but sadly numbers are down due to poor management and rampant poaching in the 1980s and the early 1990s. Kafue offers a variety of camps and lodges, some of which are attractively priced.

In recent years, there have been concerted efforts to restore the park to its former glory, which are starting to pay off. Kafue is reawakening as one of Zambia's premier parks. Lodges are being upgraded and even the park's elephants are starting to recover from the bloody slaughter of the 1980s.

Forming part of Zambia's high central plateau, Kafue is between 970 and 1,470 metres above sea level and has several distinct eco-systems: riverine forests, miombo woodland, mopane woodland, teak forests, savannah and wetlands.

In the far north of the park, which is divided by the main road into northern and southern sectors, is Kafue's jewel in the crown: the Busanga Plains, a vast tract of grassland, a seasonal floodplain accessible only between late July and November dotted with wild fig trees and wild date palms and covered by huge herds of the water-loving and near-endemic red lechwe, pukus and solitary grazers such as roan antelope and oribis.

With the coming of the dry season, buffalo, zebra and wildebeest, whose migration to the plains in September is the second largest migration in Africa, move on to the perfect grazing plains.

This in turn attracts the predators, especially lions, hyenas and wild dogs. Kafue is also one of the best places in Zambia to see leopards, which are regularly spotted on night drives.

Very few tourists visit the Busanga Plains; they are very remote and accessible only for a few months of the year but the long trip to them is definitely worth it. The swaying grasslands seem to go on forever - in many ways they are the quintessential image of Africa - and they are one of the most impressive game-viewing areas in the whole of Zambia.

In the southern sector, vegetation is thicker, making it more difficult to see animals, although the thick woodland near the Ngoma park headquarters and information post is reportedly one of the best places to see elephants.

The calm expanse of Lake Itezhi-Tezhi, is a wonderful place to enjoy fishing and glorious sunsets. The lake can be reached easily. It has a number of lodges and camps dotted around its edge which, unlike places in the more remote areas, often can accommodate walk-in customers.

In the deep, remote south is the fascinating Nanzhila Plains, which, like Busanga in the north, are home to the red lechwe, roan and sable antelopes, hartebeest and buffalos. Kafue is a rich and exciting treasure trove of bird life, with close to 450 species supported by the park's different habitats.

The not-easy-to-spot Pel's fishing owls, purple-crested louries, African fish eagles, different types of kingfishers, bee-eaters, cranes, storks, ibises, skimmers, the shy African finfoot and, in the Busanga Plains the rare Stanley's bustard and kori bustard, the world's heaviest flying bird, have all been recorded.

HOW TO GET THERE

Most travellers travel west from Lusaka on the main Lusaka to Mongu road, which is tarred with recent rehabilitation works.

The park entrance is nearly 300km west of Lusaka. There is an alternative route, the loop road from Livingstone, which, if it's in reasonable condition, makes a beautiful and fascinating journey.

Check for the latest information with local operators. Air charters can be arranged to the more remote camps.

Busanga Trails runs transfers from Lusaka about three times a week to its camps, **Lufupa** and **Shumba Bushcamp**. Busanga also offers a special deal for backpackers, picking them up from the bus drop-off at Kafue Hook Bridge.

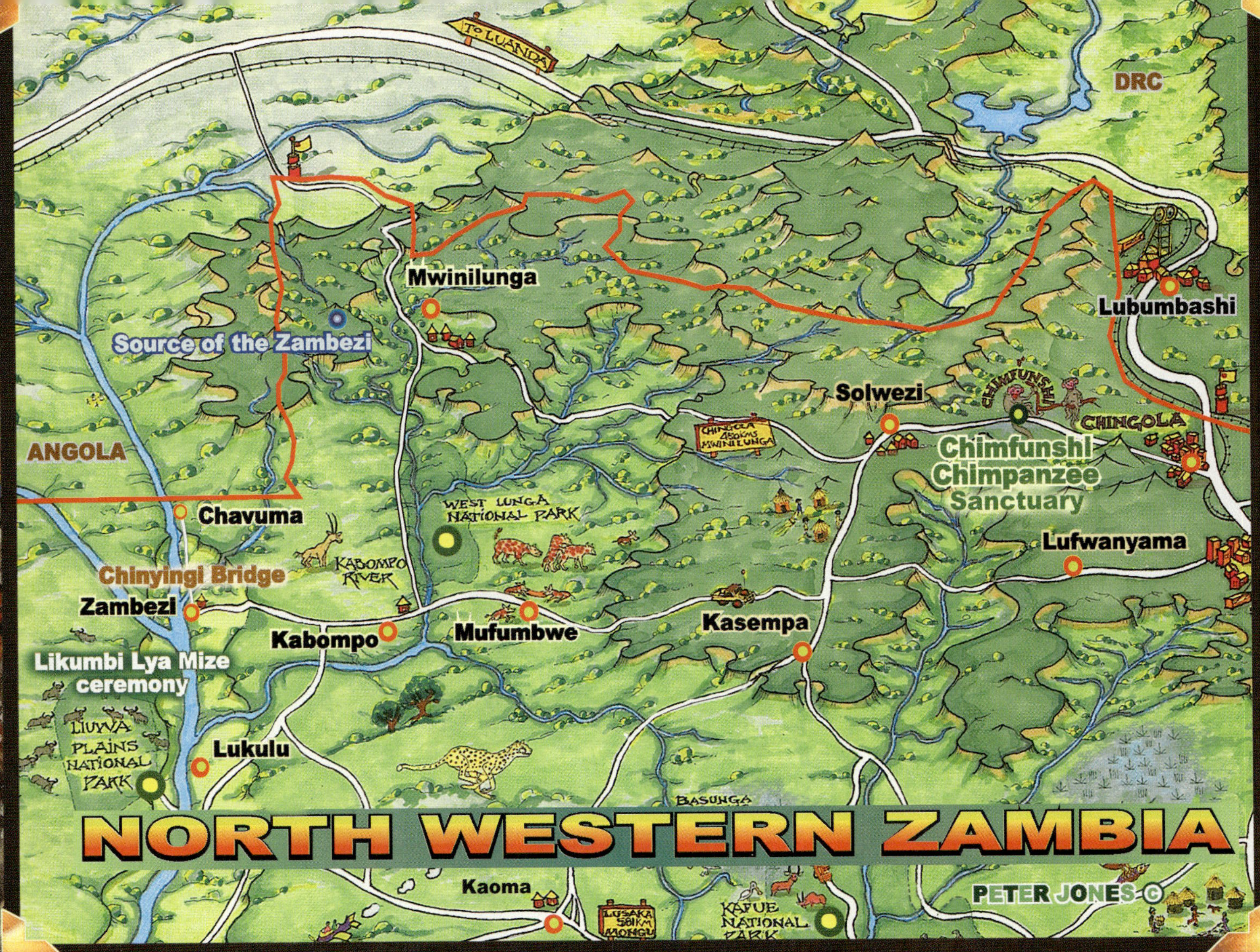

To Luanda
DRC
Mwinilunga
Lubumbashi
Source of the Zambezi
Solwezi
Chimfunshi
Chingola
Chimfunshi Chimpanzee Sanctuary
Chingola Solwezi Mwinilunga
ANGOLA
Chavuma
West Lunga National Park
Lufwanyama
Chinyingi Bridge
Kabompo River
Zambezi
Kasempa
Kabompo
Mufumbwe
Likumbi Lya Mize ceremony
Liuwa Plains National Park
Lukulu
Basunga
NORTH WESTERN ZAMBIA
Kaoma
Lusaka 581km Mongu
Kafue National Park
PETER JONES ©

THINGS TO DO

Lunga Canoe Adventure
Email: afex@super-hub.com
Takes you down the remote Lunga River in canoes, camping each night in bow tents. A beautiful experience to live so close to nature, very peaceful and relaxing.

PLACES TO STAY

Top Range

Busanga Bush Camp
Tel: (+873) 762 093 985
Email: afex@super-hub.com
Website: www.experienceafrica.com
Located on a Fig Tree Island in the middle of the Busanga Plains.

Lunga River Lodge
Tel: +(873) 762 093 985
Email: afex@super-hub.com
Website: www.experienceafrica.com
The lodge offers thatched ensuite chalets, with an appealing bar on a sundeck suspended over the river, an elevated dining room, plunge pool, steam room & massage facility. Extreme luxury and tranquility in remote natural surroundings.

Nanzhila Tented Camp
Tel: (03) 324452
Email: chundukwa@zamnet.zm
In the southern part of the park, in the heart of the bush with chalets overlooking a beautiful lagoon. Ideal base for walking and birding. safaris run from Livingstone by Chundukwa River Camp.

KAFUE National Park

Busanga Plains

Kabanga post

Masozhi post

Shumba Bush Camp

Lupemba post

Ntemwa

Moshi

Lufupa

Kafue post

Tatayoyo gate

Kafwala

Nalusanga gate

To Mongu and Western Zambia

Mukambi Safari Lodge

To Lusaka

Chunga Safari Camp

Lokomeshi post

Puku Pans

Mwenga

Kafue River

○ **Post**

◉ **Camp / Lodge**

Itumbi

Itezhi Tezhi Dam

Itezhitezhi post

New Kalala

David Shepard Camp

Musungwa Lodge

Ngoma

Ibulamushi post

Nanzhila

Kalenje post

Dumdumwenze gate

PETER JONES ©

Shumba Camp
Tel: (01) 227739-40, Fax: (01) 223724
Email: sblagus@zamnet.zm
Web: www.busangatrails.com
Spectacular location on Busanga Plains with chalets built to blend in with the surroundings. Wonderful viewing platform.

Middle Range

Lufupa Lodge
Tel: (01) 227739-40, Fax: (01) 223724
Email: sblagus@zamnet.zm
Well-established lodge built next to the Kafue River in a beautiful location, offering spacious ensuite thatched chalets and self-catering house for up to 12 people. Comfortable, informal, good choice for middle range and budget travellers.

McBrides Camp, Tel (01)252476/ 252657
Email: lubungu@zamnet.zm
Spectacular outlook of the kafue River.

Mukambi Safari Lodge
Tel: (097) 800651
Email: mukambi@zamnet.zm
Web:www..mukambi.com
Only 4 hours from Lusaka, turn left before Kafue bridge, well sign-posted. Ten chalets overlooking the water, pool area & terrace with splendid views across the river to the Miombo forest.
Tented bush camp available for self-catering.

Musungwa Safaris, Tel: (01) 273493
/274233, Fax: (01) 274233/273207
Email: zamker@zamnet.zm
Scenic lake view with picturesque sunsets. Offers camp sites, boat trips and game drives.

Puku Pan Lodge, Tel: (01) 263395
/263082, Cell:(097) 780080,
Fax: (01) 263083
Email: pukupan@zamnet.zm
Web: www.pukupan.com
Puku Pan is a unique lodge on the Kafue river. Approximately, six hours drive or a 40-minute flight from Lusaka, located deep in brachystegia woodland that is broken by extraordinarily shaped kopjes. Transport from Lusaka can be arranged.

MONGU

For the Kuomboka, which usually takes place around Easter time, visitors will need to get to Mongu, the administrative centre of Western Province. Mongu has a variety of government offices, fuel stations, shops, a few hotels and a market. Located on the edge of the Zambezi floodplain, 25km from the Zambezi River, Mongu is usually a quiet place, but during the Kuomboka it bursts with life.

On the outskirts of Mongu is Limulunga, which is the royal winter capital complete with the Litunga's modern palace. At Limulunga there is also the interesting Nayuma museum, which has a collection of artefacts from western Zambia. The Litunga, the ruler of Lozi tribe who dominate in the area, stays here when the Zambezi River floods the plains on which the summer capital of Lealui is built.

Lealui, more of a traditional village than Limulunga, lies about 32km southeast of Mongu on the flood plain. To get there and see the departure of the Litunga, you have to travel by boat.

The flood plains near Mongu are beautiful and, accompanied by a local guide, are worth exploring. On the floodplains itself, the Lozi people have built an intricate network of canals, which can be explored by canoe. The fishing in this area is highly recommended, but do bring along all the equipment you require. For Mongu, carry on the same road, travelling through Kaoma, the last fuel stop before Mongu.

Buses, including the occasional luxury one, also run from Lusaka to Mongu. It's worth paying the small extra amount of money and making sure the coach you get on is in fact the luxury one, the journey is a long one, between 8 and 11 hours.

PLACES TO STAY

Lumba Guest House, Tel: (07) 221287, 8 self-contained rooms, with restaurant and outside bar. Outside of Mongu on the way from Lusaka.

Lyambai Hotel, Tel: (07) 221138, Fax: (07) 221138
Basic facilities.

Ngulu Hotel, Tel: (07) 221258, Fax: (07) 221286
A good hotel possibly the best on offer in Mongu, situated on Senanga Rd, overlooking the floodplains. 18 rooms, with 5 executive suites, the rest are doubles with ensuite facilities, a restaurant and cocktail bar.

THE WILD WEST

Lukanga Swamp

Mumbwa

Kafue flood plain

Monze

Choma

LIVINGSTONE 472KM LUSAKA

Kalomo

Zimba

Livingstone

Kafue flood plain

LAKE ITEZHI TEZHI

BASANGA PLAINS

KAFUE NATIONAL PARK

LIVINGSTONE 525KM MONGU

Mulobezi

MOSI-OB-TUNYA NATIONAL PARK

KASANE

Kazungula

SESEKA 58KM MONGU

Kaoma

Katima Mulilo

Sesheke

NAMIBIA

Limulunga

MONGU

Ngonye Falls

Senanga

Lealui

Kuomboka Festival

Lukulu

SIOMA NGWEZI NATIONAL PARK

Sioma

The Zambezi Flood Plains

Kalabo

ZAMBEZI RIVER

Shangombo

LIUYA PLAINS NATIONAL PARK

PETER JONES ©

Sir Mwanawina Motel

Tel: (07) 221485, Fax: (07) 221856
The motel is situated on the Lealuyi Plains overlooking the palace. Has basic accomodation with restaurant and bar.

Mongu Lodge, Tel: (07) 221501,
Fax: (07) 221501
Within town and offers basic facilities.

LIUWA PLAINS NATIONAL PARK

Liuwa comprises 3,666 sq km of vast grassy plains watered by the Luambimba and Luanginga rivers.

The park is the only national park in which people are allowed to settle due to an old agreement between the central government and the Lozi traditional ruler, the Litunga.

Liuwa's main attractions are the migration of the blue wildebeest which takes place at the start of the rainy season in about November or December and its huge black-maned lions, thought to be the biggest in Zambia.

The park is extremely remote and there are very few facilities for visitors, except the Mata Manene Safari Camp, which needs to be booked in advance.

If travelling independently, you have to organise a game scout from the ZAWA office in Kalabo, about 80km from Mongu and 30km from the park.

Take absolutely everything you may think you will need and bear in mind that you will also have to provide for the ZAWA scout.

Mata Manene Safari Camp

Tel: +(27) 82 338 0896/680 9876,
Fax: +(27) 11 460 0161/082 131 338 0896
Email: zambezia@mweb.co.za
Website: www.afrika-safari.com
The only safari camp in this remote area. Guests are accommodated in 6 luxury safari tents with ensuite facilities.

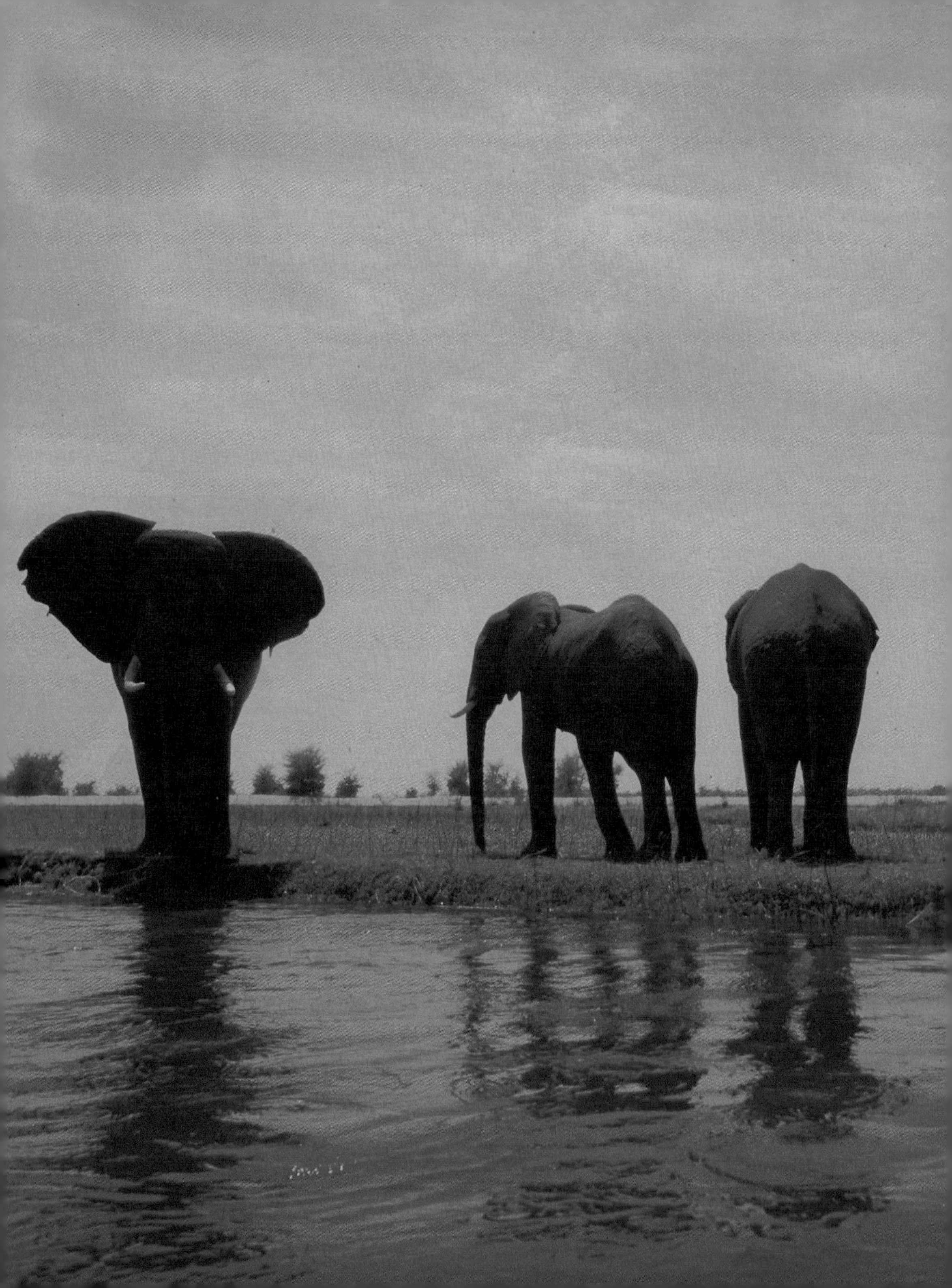

THE BAOBAB IN SUNSET

KARIBA AND LOWER ZAMBEZI

Formed in the 1960s, Lake Kariba is one of the largest artificial lakes in the world. The controversy over the flooding of the Gwembe Valley straddling Zambia and Zimbabwe, which displaced over 60,000 Tonga people, rumbles on today. While the massive Operation Noah was launched to rescue wild animals trapped on islands by the rising water, the lake's legacy to the displaced people was not so impressive.

As well as being a source of electricity, Kariba is an important commercial fishing centre, although stocks of the small kapenta fish have declined due to over fishing.

The dam is named after a huge rock buttress called Kariba which local Tonga people believe is the home of their river god – the fish-headed and serpent-tailed Nyaminyami.

The myth goes that the dam is cursed because Nyaminyami's resting place was disturbed by construction work. Certainly, the dam has been plagued by a series of problems: two major floods two years running during the construction, choking Kariba weed which at one stage covered up to a third of the lake and threatened to block the dam's outlet, and more recently drought, rumours of earth tremors and cracks in the dam.

Siavonga is the main town that sprawls along the Zambian side of Lake Kariba. There's not much going on in the town itself: there's a couple of shops and a market. Along the lake shores, however, are half a dozen or so hotels, lodges and camps that make for a refreshing and relaxing weekend break, especially for Lusaka dwellers. It offers a bit more tranquillity than you may find over in the Zimbabwean side where the busy tourist town of Kariba boasts larger resort-like hotels and a yacht marina.

A trip to Kariba Dam is worthwhile. Eagle's Rest arranges visits into the underground power station, where you can see the massive turbine halls. Otherwise, you can go through the border post, telling the officials that you don't intend to go into Zimbabwe so that your visa is not affected, and peer into the depths below from the dam walls.

Boat rides on the lake are popular, with most hotels and lodges offering sunset cruises or you can spend longer on the water by hiring a house boat for a few days.

Also, worth a visit is the crocodile farm, especially at feeding time. Downstream from Kariba Dam is Kariba Gorge, a remote area of rocky escarpments and rapids ideal for a canoe safari.

HOW TO GET THERE

By Road

Take the main road south from Lusaka to Chirundu, which winds its way through wooded Zambezi escarpment, a spectacular sight, which can be dangerous given the number of loaded lorries that use this route.

After about 120km, turn right at the signpost for Siavonga. It is then a further 60km to Siavonga.

OPENING OF THE GATES- KARIBA DAM

SIAVONGA AND LAKE KARIBA

184 KMS to LUSAKA

PRICES BANANA FARM

TAMARIND CAMP

ZAMBEZI GORGE

ZIMBABWE

350 KMS to HARARE

NORTH

KARIBA TOWN

KARIBA STORE

DUBBLERS FISHING SAFARIS

LOTTERY BAY

BANANA ISLAND

GWENA ISLAND

MPANGO PENINSULA

SIAVONGA HARBOUR

DAM WALL

RHINO ISLAND

SAMPA KARTUMA ISLAND GROUP

FOTHERGILL ISLAND

ZEBRA ISLAND

ANTELOPE ISLAND

REDCLIFFE ISLAND

TSETSE ISLAND

LAKE KARIBA

15 KM HOUSE BOAT

1½ HOURS BY SPEED BOAT

20 MINUTES BY

PETER JONES ©

A - Eagle's Rest Lodge

B - Manchichi Bay lodge

C - Leisure Bay Lodge

D - Lake Safari Lodge

E - Lake Kariba Inn

F - Crocodile Farm

G - North Bank Guest House

H - Petrol

I - Mitchel's Clinic

J - Zambian Border Post

K - Zimbabwean Border Post

L - Inchinga Trails (C/S)

M - Sandy Bay (Camp Site - C/S)

VIEW FROM THE DAM WALL

Middle Range

Top Range

Chete Island Safari Lodge
Tel (27 11) 886 9232/9234,
Fax (27 11) 781 0165/0483
Email: reservations@cheteisland.com
Web: www.cheteisland.com
This lodge is on Lake Kariba. Access by road through Sinazongwe, sign posted at Batoka which is on-route between Lusaka and Livingstone, catmarine across the lake. Spacious Kenyan Meru style safari tents. Each under cool thatch with ensuite bathrooms, elegant mahogany furniture.

Lake Kariba Inns, Tel (01) 253768 /511269, Fax (01) 252518 /511188
Accessed through Siavonga town, turn right before the harbour well sign-posted. Conference facilities available and enticing swimming pool with a games room for the children. Set high on the hill overlooking the lake. All rooms are ensuite. Public telephone. Boat cruises and floating sundowners can be arranged through the Inn.

Sandy Beach Safari,
Tel (01) 231936/511168,
Fax (01) 231936 /511168
Email:eagles@zamnet.zm
On the route to Siavonga, signposted turnoff on the right, friendly lodge, famous for its sandy secluded beach on the shores of Lake Kariba, offering a variety of accommodation options from fullboard, to self-catering or camping.

Lake Safari Lodge, Tel (01) 511148 /511024, Fax (01) 511029
Email: info@lakesafari.com
Located in Siavonga town just adjacent to the harbour. Picturesque hotel on the lakeshore with a swimming pool.

Manchichi Bay Lodge, Tel (01) 236693/ 222681, Fax (01) 236689
Email: manchim@zamnet.zm
Easy access on tarred road, well sign posted turn off before Siavonga town.
Air-conditioned lodge on the shores of Lake Kariba set on a peninsula with a bay adjacent for mooring boats. Conference facilities available and swimming pool.

Chikanka Island
Tel (032) 20169 /20021 /20119,
Fax (032) 20054 / 20570,
Cell (097) 803292 / 777719, Lake Kariba
Email:gwemsaf@coppernet.zm,
Web: www.zambiatourism.com/gwembe
A privately owned Island. Access is via Sinazongwe, sign posted at Batoka which is on-route between Lusaka and Livingstone. It lies about 12km west/south west of Chete Island Game Sanctuary in Kariba. Hosts a wide variety of game.

Budget

Eagles Rest, Tel (01) 511168/ 231936
Email: eagles@zamnet.zm
Web: www.eagles-rest.com
Signposted off Siavonga road, located after Manchichi Bay. Offers accommodation with options for self catering chalets and camping facilities on the lake front. Bar, restaurant and swimming pool. A wide variety of activities can be arranged including canoeing and safaris on Lower Zambezi

Leisure Bay Lodge
Tel (01) 51135/6, Fax (01) 511136
Located on the bank of Lake Kariba access is from Lake Drive road, well sign posted. Comfortable accommodation with a lovely view of the lake.

Kariba North Bank
Tel (01) 511197/ 511237/ 511521 ,
Fax (01) 511197
Email: knbc@zamnet.zm
Located on the top of the hill with a breathtaking view of the lake especially the sunrise and sunset. Air-conditioned and self-contained bedrooms with satellite TV.

Tamarind Camp
Tel (01) 231936,
 Fax (01) 231936
Email: eagles@zamnet.zm
Wesite: www.eagles-rest.com
Self catering camp comprising with tents under thatched roofs. Fully equipped kitchen. Bedding is provided, but best to bring your own. Brings you closer to nature.

Chete Island
SAFARI LODGE
LAKE KARIBA, ZAMBIA

A chain of islands lies hidden away in the western reaches of Lake Kariba - these are the Westlake islands. When the great Zambezi River filled Kariba, it became the largest man made lake in the world. The islands have remained remote and untouched since 1959, offering a unique setting for the newly built Chete Island deluxe tented Safari Lodge.

ACTIVITIES:
- Canoe game viewing
- Motorised boat game viewing cruises
- Sailing Cruises
- Day and Night game drives in an open Landrover
- Game walks with an armed professional Game Ranger
- Bush barbecues and Champagne breakfasts
- Night Sky Observation of the Milky Way Galaxy with a high quality Astronomical Telescope

- Fishing by boat or canoe in pursuit of the famous fighting Zambezi Tiger fish
- Bird watching in a National Bird Sanctuary
- Radio communication with mainland
- Daily laundry services
- Lighting by solar power and paraffin lamps
- Access to medical air rescue service
- Swimming pool

Reservations & Information: Tel: +27 11 886 9232/9234 Fax: + 27 11 781 0165/0483 e-mail: reservations@cheteisland.com Website: RSA www.cheteisland.co.zaINTL.: www.cheteisland.com

THINGS TO DO

Boating

Tiger Trails, Tel (01) 511108 *Email: tigerpiet@zamnet.zm* Spacious houseboat fully serviced with self catering option.

Canoeing

Canoe trips starting from the base of the Kariba Dam, travelling down river to the Lower Zambezi National Park, staying at the various camps.

Game Viewing

River Horse Safaris, Tel (01) 511107 /263 61 2447/2944, Fax 263 61 2944/2422; *Email: riverhse@mweb.co.zw; Web: www.riverhorse.co.zw* and

Sobek, Tel (01) 231936, Fax(01) 231936, *Email: anderson@zamnet.zm; Web: www.eagles-rest.com*

BATELEUR HOUSE BOAT

LAKE KARIBA SIAVONGA ZAMBIA

5 BEDROOMS (SLEEPS 10 0R MORE)
TAILOR YOUR GROUP TO YOUR OWN REQUIREMENTS
ALL AMENITIES (Toilets, Showers)
*SELF CATERING   *TENDER BOAT & EQUIPMENT   *BAR   *BRAII

Contact: TIGER TRAILS
TEL: 09-260-1-511108
email: tigerpiet@zamtel.zm

LOWER ZAMBEZI

If you're looking for breath-taking beauty, the Lower Zambezi National Park will not disappoint you. It is one of Zambia's if not Africa's top wildlife parks and covers 4000sq km on the northern bank of the wide and mighty Zambezi River. Across the water is the famous, world heritage site of Mana Pools in Zimbabwe.

On the Zambian side, the park is going from strength-to-strength and a trip to Zambia would not be complete without getting a taste of one of the most special places in the country.

The Lower Zambezi is a spectacular grassy flood plain dappled with thickets and clusters of Africa's quintessential acacia trees, edged on the northern side by hills and a steep escarpment covered with thick miombo woodland.

The escarpment is especially impressive when the lowering sun turns it into a shadow of blue and pink. The southern border is the Zambezi river. Several smaller rivers flow through the park and there are numerous pans and swamp areas.

The main entrance gate is the Chongwe Gate on the western boundary of the park, heading from the border town of Chirundu. The south-western part of the park is both scenic and accessible; as a consequence most camps and lodges are located here.

As you go further into the park, it becomes wilder. At the eastern boundary is the dramatic Mpata Gorge, where the steep hill plunges straight into the river and the only access is by boat, usually from Luangwa. Here the flood plain which dominates much of the park has given way to hills.

The Zambezi River is dotted with islands, some no more than rocky out-crops, others more impressive sandbanks on which crocs and hippos sun themselves while towering hulks of jackleberry, mahogany and winterthorn trees line the river.

Animals tend to congregate on the flood plain and along the river, meaning that river trips are one of the best and most exciting ways to see all sorts of wildlife in the Lower Zambezi.

Most of the camps and lodges have canoes and boats so you can go out with an experienced river guide for a few hours either for a lazy day on the river, watching hippos up close, crocodiles, buffalo and elephant or brightly coloured bee-eaters as they make their nests in the sandy riverbanks.

The elephant population is making a comeback, and it's not uncommon to see the moving sight of up to 50 animals in one herd, making the river crossing or simply frolicking in the water. The elephants are much bigger than those in Luangwa.

Large herds of buffalo are also common here, so don't be surprised if driving through thickets you have to give way to a crowd making their dusty way across the road.

The park's small but growing African wild dog population was once almost wiped out by disease, but you now have a good chance of seeing these black and yellow dappled animals. Other mammal species in the park include puku, impala, zebra, bushbuck, lion, leopard and cheetah.

There are more than 400 bird species, including the unusual African skimmer and narina trogon.

Fishing in the Lower Zambezi is one of the best in Zambia and finally after years of exploitation it is now strictly controlled. Longer canoe safaris are also possible (see National Parks section page 49) and are one of the activities that make the Lower Zambezi one of the more popular destinations in Zambia.

HOW TO GET THERE

By Air

Chartered flights to Lower Zambezi can be arranged through the local travel agents. Otherwise, lodges will arrange air travel, either to the Jeki airstrip which is a 40 minute flight from Lusaka, or their own strips, and a transfer to the lodge. Places to stay at the eastern side are reached via Luangwa town, although transfers to Kingfisher Camp and Redcliff Lodge, included in the price, are by boat only.

By Road

Driving to the Lower Zambezi is much more of an option than driving to Luangwa Valley. For a start, it's only five hours or so from Lusaka but the road is inaccessible in the rainy season (November to April) and many lodges close. Even in the dry season you'd need 4WD and high clearance.

From Chirundu, turn left on to a dirt road signposted Gwabi Lodge. If you are driving the whole way, do not turn off to Gwabi but instead carry straight to cross the Kafue River using the delightfully old-fashioned but sturdy pontoon. About 80kms from Chirundu is the main Chongwe Gate.

By Boat

You can also access the park and lodges, which all look over the river, by boat from Gwabi Lodge.
Tel: (01) 515078,
Fax: (01) 515062
Email: gwabi@zamnet.zm.
It is only 2 hours from Lusaka, easy to get to on a good road. But this lodge is still some distance from the park and therefore its comfortable chalets built next to the Kafue river are a good stop-over point either for travellers into the park or for a weekend break. You can leave your car and be picked up by boat to lodges in the Lower Zambezi.

PLACES TO STAY

Top Range

Royal Zambezi Lodge,
Tel: (01) 274901/096 861020,
Fax: (01) 274901,
Email: rzl@zamnet.zm,
Website: www.lionroars.com
On the banks of the Lower Zambezi river, about 10km from the Park entry gate. By road it is approximately one hour from the pontoon.

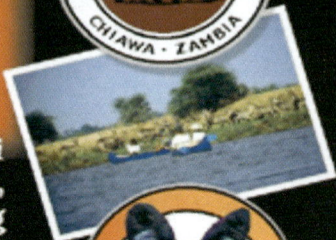

196

Mwambashi River Lodge
Tel: (01) 272359 (263 4) 700911 / 700912 / 700707,
Fax: (01) 274901
Email:rzl@zamnet.zm
Web: www.zambezisafari.com;
Situated in the heart of the Lower Zambezi National Park on the Northern banks of the river, directly opposite Chikwenya Island and the eastern boundary of the Mana Pools National Park. Access by charter to Jeki airstrip from Livingstone, Lusaka and Mfuwe, by road or boat, clients are transported by boat approximately three hours from the Kafue pontoon.

Chiawa Camp, Tel: (01) 261588,
Fax: (01) 262683
Email: info@chiawa.comb
Website: www.chiawa.com
Luxury safari lodge on the banks of the Zambezi river. Safari tented chalets with ensuite bathroom. Upstairs thatched lounge area. Approximately one and half hours drive from Jeki air strip.

Kanyemba Lodge, Tel: (01) 265836,
Fax: (01) 260012
Email: info@kanyemba.com
Website: www.kanyemba.com
Roomy and comfortable thatched chalets have private verandas overlooking the river, all ensuite bathroom. Has a wonderful patio and a library

Kasakasaka Luxury Tented Camp
Tel: (01) 265836/ 260313,
Fax: (01) 260012
Email: nyamsaf@coppernet.zm
Website: www.kasakasaka.com
About six km from the Lower Zambezi National Park boundary lies this small, exclusive camp overlooking the Zambezi River. The chalets including the honeymoon suite are connected by elevated walkways allowing a birdseye view of the elephants which often wander into the camp. Large tamarind trees shade the dining and bar areas. Swimming pool.

Kayila Lodge
Tel: (263 4) 700911 / 700912 / 700707,
Fax: (263 4) 706318
Email: speres@mweb.co.zw
Web: www.zambezisafari.com
Situated on a private wildlife sanctuary approximately 45 km from Chirundu. Beautiful thatched chalets, a honeymoon suite and a treehouse built 30 feet up in a sausage tree. Offers magnificent views of the river and escarpment. Baobab tree with interesting ablutions. Swimming pool.

Kiambi Safari Lodge
Tel: +27 31 563 9774, Fax: +27 31 563 1957
Email: Karibu@karibu.co.za
Web: www.karibu.co.za
Located on the banks of the Zambezi River in front of the Kanyemba Island and Hurungwe safari area. Tented rooms on raised wooden platforms with ensuite facilities and private verandas. A bar under thatch with a raised deck overlooking the Zambezi River. Small swimming pool. Sunset cruise, canoeing, stargazing (April to December), birdwatching.

Kiubo River Lodge, Tel: +27 31 563 9774, Fax: +27 31 563 1957
Email: Karibu@karibu.co.za
Web: www.karibu.co.za
Situated on the northern banks of the Zambezi River. The wide, elevated river frontage provides wonderful views to wards Mana Pools. Game viewing by boat and canoe. Tented rooms on raised wooden platforms, ensuite facilities and private verandas. Bar & dining area under spectacular giant ebony tree. Swimming pool.

Kulefu Game Lodge, Tel:+263 9 471225/ 471750/4, Fax: +263 9 471715
Email: info@starofafrica.co.zw
Web: www.star-of-africa.com
Set on a small channel of the Zambezi River, in the secluded heart of the Lower Zambezi National Park. Kulefu sprawls in the deep shade of towering acacia trees, while the river gently unfolds on its doorstep. Comprising of ensuite tented rooms on raised platforms, and private verandas. Game-viewing on land (May to December); game-viewing by boat and canoe (January to December), birdwatching; stargazing (April to December).

Mvuu Lodge,
Tel : +27 16 987 1837/ +27 83 277 3031
Fax: 27 16 987 2655
Email: info@mvuulodge.com
Website: www.mvuulodge.com
Located about 65 km from Chirundu in the Chiawa Game Management area, set against the beautiful Chirundu escarpment fronted by the Zambezi river. Luxury chalets, with thatched roofs on raised wooden decks. Self catering available in exclusive campsite with hot shower, flush toilets and basin in reed enclosures.

The River House, Tel (263) 91 236019 (263) 91 240852 (260) 97 227222,
Email: hannes@icon.co.zw
Web: www.zambezia.com
Campsite with a convential type house, ideal for families.

Sausage Tree Camp
Tel : (01) 272456, Fax: (01) 272456
Email: info@sausagetreecamp.com
Website: www.sausagetreecamp.com
The camp is nestled amongst mature mahogany, acacia and sausage trees. It is high on the riverbank overlooking scenic channels dotted with water lilies and pods of hippo. Sausage Tree specializes in offering a very personalized experience in luxurious ensuite bedouin-style tents.

Middle Range

Chongwe River Camp, Tel: (097) 772905/ 02 512814, Fax: 02 510360
Email: atd@zamnet.zm
On the confluence of the Zambezi and Chongwe rivers and only 10 minutes from the game park, this camp has possibly one of the best sites in the park. Accommodates up to 14 guests in spacious tented chalets with ensuite facilities. The emphasis is changing from self-catering to catered and upmarket, although the owner is keen not to do away with all self-catering facilities.

Mtondo Fishing & Safari Lodge
Tel (263) 91 236019 (263) 91 240852 (260) 97 227222,
Email: hannes@icon.co.zw
Web: www.zambezia.com
Fully equiped ensuite chalets under thatch, simple, spacious and comfortable.

Shafumbi Mountain Camp

Tel (263) 91 236019 (263) 91 240852 (260) 97 227222

Email: hannes@icon.co.zw,
Web: www.zambezia.com

Well ventilated double ensuite tented chalets situated on a small hill at the base of mountains. It is beautifully shaded by massive tamarind trees and commands a fabulous view of the Zambezi flood plain.

Kingfisher Lodge

Tel: (01) 290146 (096) 751302/ 761271, Fax: (01) 295546

Email; rshenton@zamnet.zm

Outside the park's eastern boundary, only accessible by boat from Luangwa town, this small and relaxed camp offers a wonderful riverside setting, fishing and boat trips to the stunning Mpata Gorge or further upriver for walking safaris where you can see different animals.

Redcliff Zambezi Lodge, Tel: +27 12 653 2664, Fax: +27 12 654 4015

Email: 4tigers@bushmail.net
andreb@solo.pipex.co.za
Website: www.redcliff-lodge.com

Access by only boat only, ensuite chalets, excellent fishing options.

Budget

Kwalata Camp

Email: kachelo@zamnet.zm

24 kms from the pontoon, camp site with ablution block, kitchen area with freezer and fridge. Take own tents and cooking equipment.

Samango Camp, Tel: (01) 231 936, Fax: (01) 231936

Located on the banks of the Zambezi River accessed from the Eastern gate. Ideal for group camps.

Kiboko Adventures
Tel: +27 31 5639774,
Fax: +27 31 563 1957
Email: karibusa@iafrica.com
Website:www.karibu.co.za
Offers game drives, game viewing by boat, fishing and sundowner cruises.

Safari Par Excellence
Tel: (263 4) 700911 / 700912 / 700707,
Fax: (263 4) 706318
Email: speres@mweb.co.zw
Web: www.safariparexcellence.com
Safari Par Excellence conducts mobile backed up walking safaris in the Lower Zambezi between the Chongwe River and Mwambashi River lodge.

KALAMBO FALLS

NORTHERN WATERS

NORTHERN ZAMBIA

Those who take time to explore the north of Zambia will find much to delight and astonish. It's a huge area and one of the most beautiful places in Zambia: there are hills, valleys, lakes, rivers, wetlands and waterfalls galore. It is not usually on the itinerary of most visitors due to the remoteness and poor access. Thanks to the region's numerous rivers and rolling landscape, it nurtures about 20 spectacular waterfalls, more than any other province in the country.

Most are off the main roads and so visitors will need a vehicle, although the best falls, Chishimba, Lumangwe and Kalambo, are all reachable by public transport and hitching. Here too is Lake Tanganyika, the longest freshwater lake on the planet.

A beautiful place where you can either idle away hours on the shimmering water, or take up the challenge of some of the most demanding freshwater fishing in Africa. Or there is Kasanka National Park, a small but delightful place. Northern Zambia also holds one of Africa's most important wetland areas - the vast Bangweulu wetlands or swamps, a magical place.

MKUSHI

This small town in the heart of beautiful rolling farmland is a handy transit point to refuel and stock up for the journey up north. With shops, banks, Tazara train station and petrol stations, Mkushi is just off the Great North Road.

Sweetwater Guest House Tel: (05) 362245/362217, Fax: (05) 362245, *Email: sweetwtr@zamnet.zm*; 120km from Kapiri Mposhi off Great North Road well sign posted. 6 double rooms & 1 family room all en-uite. Situated on a commercial farm in a beautiful spot overlooking the delightful Mkushi River Valley. **Forest Inn,** Tel: (05) 362003, Fax: (05) 362188, *Email: forestin@zamnet.zm* About 30km south of Mkushi turnoff, a comfortable lodge in delightful surroundings on the Great North Road. Thatched ensuite, mosquito-proof family rooms,

NTUMBACHUSHI FALLS

double & singles. Camping with BBQ & hot showers. Badminton, volleyball & croquet.

SERENJE

The next stop is Serenje, an unremarkable town although, when in season around December, the market boasts some of the best mushrooms in Zambia at bargain prices. You do not need to go into town; there's a fuel station on the road, a shop, the basic Siga Siga Motel and a local restaurant with a terrace where, if you're backpacking, you can sit and wait for the bus.

KASANKA NATIONAL PARK

For Kasanka National Park, a real gem of a park, turn left about 40km from Serenje off the Great North Road on to the Mansa road. Travel for a further 54km, then turn left at the clearly signposted into the park. Kasanka is Zambia's only privately managed national park and, covering about 400sq km of woodland and grasslands dotted with swampy areas, one of its smallest. Revenue from visitors has reinvested into the beautiful wilderness.

Kasanka is an absolutely delightful place and a few days here is highly recommended. Highlights include drifting down the river watching all sorts of birds, such as kingfishers, Ross louries and red-and-blue sunbirds, and climbing 18metres into a viewing platform in the branches of a huge tree to search the papyrus reeds for the water-loving reddish-brown sitatunga. Kasanka is one of the best places in Africa to see these rare and extremely shy and unusual antelopes. The sitatunga has evolved splayed and elongated hooves, which allow it to walk on marshy ground without sinking. It is a good swimmer and when frightened will often submerge itself, leaving only its nostrils exposed.

Kasanka is also famous for its huge colony giant of migratory straw-coloured fruitbats. It's a truly spectacular sight in November and December, where the biggest gathering of bats in the world assemble in their millions. As they fly off at dusk in search of food, the sky goes black. It's also possible to see elephant, warthog, baboon, vervet monkey, zebra, buffalo, bushbuck, Lichtenstein's hartebeest, reedbuck, waterbuck, sable, Sharpe's grysbok and the common duiker. As well as drives and walks in Kasanka, the Kasanka team runs tours to other highlights of the region using planes or vehicles to cover North Luangwa National Park, the Bangweulu Wetlands and the English manor house of Shiwa Ngandu.

The Kasanka team also operate bush walks and other wilderness activities in the nearby Lavushi Manda National Park and trips to the Livingstone Memorial and Chief Chitambo's Palace.

PLACES TO STAY

Budget
Luwombwa Tel: + 873 762067957, Fax: (01) 224427
Email: park@kasanka.com
Website: www.kasanka.com
Fully ensuite chalets with private verandas overlooking the river. Reached by pontoon, closed December to April.

Wasa
Tel: + 873 762067957,
Fax: (01) 222906
Email: park@kasanka.com
Website: www.kasanka.com
Thatched ensuite chalets offering double bed and single in each, overlooking open grassy area that attracts wildlife. Private verandas and ensuite facilities. Also with 5 chalets without ensuite. You might not have to move out of your shelter to see wild life but instead relax in your private verandas as the animals wander by.

LIVINGSTONE MEMORIAL

The monument, a simple obelisk topped by a cross, is built on the site of the mpundu tree, long since dead, under which David Livingstone's heart was buried in 1873 following his death at Chitambo village.

To get there, drive 10km from the Kasanka turn-off and then turn right. After about 8km, turn left at the signpost and from there it is about 25km to the monument.

SHOEBILL STORK

CHIPOMA FALLS

THE NORTHERN LAKES

Tanzania

Lake Tanganyika

KALAMBO FALLS

Mbala

Mpulungu

Sumbu National Park

Kasama

Great North Road (to Tanzania)

SHIWA NG'ANDU

LUSAKA 1003KM MBEYA

Mpika

Great North Road to Lusaka

Chambeshi River

Kalungwishi River

LAKE MWERU WANTIPA

Mweru Wantipa N.P.

Kundabwika Falls

LUMANGWE FALLS

BANGWEULU SWAMPS

LAKE MWERU

Lusenga Plain N P

Kawamba

Nchelenge

D R Congo

Mwense

Luapula River

Mansa

Samfya

PETER JONES ©

BANGWEULU WETLANDS

South-east of Lake Bangweulu lie the vast and beautiful wetlands of the same name, which are surrounded by a grassy plain, flooded during the rainy season and covered with animals. The few people who live here exist on subsistence hunting and fishing. Bangweulu, which in the local language means where the water meets the sky, is famous for the rare black lechwe - which you are guaranteed to see if you come at the right time — and one of Africa's rarest birds, the shoebill stork (see photos on page 205 & 210) - more difficult to see because of its shyness and rarity.

The best place for bird and game viewing is the Chikuni sector of the game management area, where the vast herds of black lechwe antelope, found only in Bangweulu, congregate. With long, lyre shaped horns and elongated toes adapted to the wetland, herds of up to 10,000 can be seen stretching for miles and for miles across the horizon and heard as they splash through the marshes. Few places in the world contain such large antelope herds. The best time to see them is between May and July as the water starts to recede, though August to October is still good.

Other antelope include oribi, sitatunga, bushbuck, reedbuck and tsessebe. Buffalo and elephant can sometimes be seen and zebra, recently re-introduced into the area, are reported to be doing well. The antelope share the wetlands with magnificent birdlife and for a better view, especially a glimpse of the rare shoebill stork, you can venture by dugout canoe into the wetlands, a maze of clear-water channels, floating islands, palm trees and lily pads.

The shoebill stork is found only in Bangweulu, in some parts of Uganda and possibly in Sudan and the Democratic Republic of Congo. What makes it stand out is its huge, shoe-shaped bill. Technically, it's not even a stork, being closer to a pelican. Shoebills perch high on palm tress or wade through reeds looking for fish, but they are extremely shy and will fly off if disturbed.

The best time for a possible glimpse of the weird-looking shoebill is when water levels are still quite high, between March and July

There's no public transport to the wetlands, so you'll have to come in your own vehicle or chartered plane. From Kasanka National Park, a dirt road goes via Lake Waka-Waka to Chikuni GMA scout post. From there, you either drive the 2km to Shoebill Camp or go by boat, depending on water levels. **Shoebill Island**, Tel: (00 873) 762067957, Fax: (01) 222906, *Email: park@kasanka.com Website: www.kasanka.com*; 70km north of Kasanka in the heart of the Bangweulu wetlands. 6 walk-in safari tents under thatch, all with private bathrooms. Bring your own food or book meals in advance. Boats can be hired, with guides, to seek shoebill storks.

SAMFYA

On the western shore of Lake Bangweulu about 10km east of the main road between Serenje and Mansa,

SHOEBILL STORK IN FLIGHT

Samfya is the hub of lake transport and has a number of bars, restaurants and guesthouses.

Probably the best place to stay is 3km outside town at the revamped government guest house now called the **Bangweulu Lodge** and run by South Africans. Here the blue lake meets pure white beach. Camping and self-catering chalets.

The lodge has links with Tiger Fish Haven, a dedicated angling camp near Twingi, south of Samfya.

To reach Samfya there is a luxury CR coach from Lusaka, minibuses or the best option would be your own transport.

MPIKA

Mpika is a busy junction town with a train station, post office, hospital, fuel stations and college. There are a few shops which are reasonably well stocked.

From Mpika it is 389km to the border with Tanzania at Nakonde. On the Great North Road 70km south of Mpika is the turn-off to Mutinondo Wilderness, a 10,000 hectare conservation area with majestic granite inselbergs, picturesque waterfalls and pristine woodlands and wetlands.

Mutinondo Wilderness Lodge has chalets with spectacular views and a secluded campsite with good facilities. They offer a wide range of activities, including horse riding, canoeing and river tubing.

For bookings contact: +870 76 2580913, email: 2mwl@bushmail.net

SHIWA N'GANDU

If you drive 100km north of Mpika on the Great North Road and turn off at the Shiwa Ngandu signpost, after a distance of 16km you'll come across perhaps one of the most startling sights in the whole of Zambia: a rambling English country manor house overlooking a shimmering lake in the middle of the African bush.

In 1914, the young colonial officer, Stewart Gore-Brown, was working on demarcating the border between Rhodesia and the Belgian Congo. His work took him to the remote Shiwa Ngandu, or the place of the crocodiles as the local Bemba people called it, with which he instantly fell in love. He bought 100,000 hectares from the local chief and began the long task of constructing an English country manor and estate. After great difficulties, lost tempers and thanks to a rich aunt in England, the building was finally completed in 1932.

Gore-Brown, an opponent of colonialism, was one of the few settler politicians who achieved popularity and respect with nationalist leaders including the country's first president Kenneth Kaunda.

When he died at the age of 84 in 1967, he was given a state funeral by the government of Zambia and a chief's traditional burial. Gore-Brown lies on a hill overlooking the lake at Shiwa.

Gore-Brown's daughter and son-in-law struggled on with the estate and campaigned against poaching in nearby

MAMBILIMA RAPIDS

North Luangwa park, until their mysterious murder in 1992.

The great house stood empty until Gore-Brown's grandsons undertook a massive restoration and opened the house to visitors in 2001. A stay is recommended and intriguing. Your guide will probably be the charming Sunday, whose father was the cook in Shiwa's halcyon days, and whose grandfather went to Britain as Gore-Brown's valet. The story of Shiwa Ngandu is brought to life by journalist Christina Lamb in the book *The Africa House*.

You can stay at the house or at the nearby Kaphyisha Springs.

KASAMA

On the Great North Road heading towards Mbala, Kasama is the main administrative town of the Northern Province. The town has several stores, banks, an airport, train station and various places to stay. Nearby are prehistoric cave paintings and spectacular waterfalls.

PLACES TO STAY

Budget

Kasama Hotel Tel: (04)221188, Fax: (04)222700, Mpika Road

Kasembo Guest House Tel: (04)222394, Fax: (04)221158. Comfortable self contained & non-self contained rooms.

Kwacha Relax Hotel Tel: (04)221124, Fax: (04)221124 Found on Mpika Road. Basic place with a maze of dim, long corridors.

Nchinchi Guest House Tel: (04)221441, Fax: (04)222279
Email: chitischool@zamtel.zm
Simple in its layout and provides all the basic amenities.

Tiya Guest House Tel: (04)222283, Fax: (04) 222283.

Thorn Tree Guest House 612 Zambia Road Tel: (04)221615, Fax: (04)221615
Email: kansato@zamnet.zm
Best and friendliest place in town, 1km beyond the Heritage Centre. Very clean, comfortable rooms set in beautiful garden. 1 cottage with bedroom, lounge, kitchen and bathroom single & double rooms. 4 large ensuite rooms. 4 rooms shared bathroom. Prices include continental breakfast. Other meals available. Communal lounge and fully stocked bar.

THINGS TO DO

Kasama's ancient treasure

About 7km east of Kasama on the road to Isoka, in cave and overhangs in the bush is one of the greatest densities of rock art sites in Southern Africa, with over 700 registered sites in a relatively small area.

Some paintings are considered by archaeologists to be amongst the most significant on the continent.

The paintings are thought to have been done by Stone Age hunter-gatherer ancestors of today's Zambians known as the Twa. Though the dating of these paintings is still debated, most experts are confident they were painted before 1000 AD.

Particularly well known are the sites at Sumina, where at the end of a steep path is a well-preserved picture of a hunter chasing a lion and a buffalo. At Mwela the paintings are mostly geometric, including rows of dots and circles. The Mwankole site has various designs including dancing people and the famous penis image. Though this art has survived for thousands of years, keep in mind that it can easily be damaged, even if you touch it lightly. The paintings are national monuments and pro-

CHISHIMBA FALLS

tected by law. There is an entrance fee of about US$3. With advance notice, you can arrange a guide with the Heritage Centre in Kasama or find the friendly caretaker at his house.

About 90km south of Kasama, at the north end of the Chambeshi River bridge is the Von Lettow Vorbeck Memorial monument, also known as the Chambeshi National Monument.

The monument marks the spot where General Von Lettow Vorbeck, the German Commander in East Africa, and his forces exchanged fire with the British-led troops in the First World War before finally surrendering to Mr Hector Croad, Mpika District Commissioner, following the German surrender and armistice of 11 November 1918.

CHISHIMBA FALLS

About 30km out on the road from Kasama to Luwingu take the right turn to Mporokoso and about 5Km up that road, you will find a turning on the left which leads to Chishimba Falls on the Luombe River, nestling in a wooded area. Chishimba Falls is actually three successive cascades: Mutumuna Falls, Keyela Falls and Chishimba Falls. Local legend has it that the Falls are inhabited by spirits. Although a hydro-electric station has been built to harness Chishimba Falls' power to generate electricity, it does not detract from the natural beauty of the falls.

LUMANGWE FALLS

To get to Lumangwe Falls from Kasama drive about 160km north to Mporokoso. But be warned the road is in a terrible state. From Mporokoso drive for another 80km on the Kawamba road to the falls. The Lumangwe Falls are certainly impressive. Covering an area of 65 hectares, the deafening roar of falling water, mists of spray and surrounding rainforest have led to its nickname as the 'mini Victoria Falls'. They are 30 metres high and over a 100 metres wide. Camping is permitted and nearby is the Cascade Cottage guesthouse.

MBALA

Mbala is a small, relaxed town, with a few reminders of its busier colonial days when it was know as Abercorn, the Tanganyika Victoria Memorial Institute, now a library and crèche, and the former Booth's Native Stores. All buses between Lusaka and Mpulungu run via Mbala. If you're on your way to Lake Tanganyika, take a break here. Enjoy the cool climate — at 5,400ft Mbala has the distinction of being the highest town in Zambia — before heading down into the severe heat of the Great Rift Valley. A trip 3km out of town to the fascinating and well-organised Moto Moto Museum (Tel 04 450098) is really worthwhile. The museum opened in 1974 and boasts perhaps the best collection in Zambia of cultural artefacts of the Bemba people.

These include a wide range of weapons, tools, household objects and musical instruments. It also houses a unique collection of Mbusa figures used in the initiation rites of Bemba girls and

MUBULUMA FALLS

a collection of Zambian and Congolese masks and statuettes. You can bring food for a picnic in the museum gardens.

PLACES TO STAY

Arms Motel   President Avenue
Tel: (04) 450585. Very basic facilities.

Christy Inn, Tel: (04) 450350
New Mbulu Road

Grasshopper Inn Tel: 04 450589
Easily accessible, off the main street. Best place in town, with clean rooms, bar and restaurant.

KALAMBO FALLS

About 40km north of Mbala are the Kalambo Falls, a magnificent 221-metre drop of water. More than twice the height of the Victoria Falls, these are the second highest single-drop waterfalls in Africa and the twelfth highest in the world. The views of the green gorge below and the horizon are breathtaking. Kalambo Falls are also a site of archaeological importance.   Here the earliest evidence of fire in Sub-Saharan Africa was found. It is also a nesting place of the rare Marabou stork. Basic camping facilities are available at the site.

MPULUNGU

About 40km from Mbala down in the rift valley on the shores of the magnificent Lake Tanganyika is Zambia's only port. Luxury coaches travel several times a week between Lusaka and Mpulungu, via Kasama and Mbala.

Mpulungu is a busy commercial port and the terminal for the steamer that links Zambia with Kigoma in eastern Tanzania and Bujumbura, the capital of Burundi.

So if you want an enterprising way to leave Zambia and one of the best ways of seeing Lake Tanganyika, pick up a passenger steamer here.   But don't expect plain sailing: the vessels are not set up for a touristy jaunt.

About 2km east of Mpulungu is Niamkolo church.   A crumbled old church, built in 1896 by the London Missionary Society, it is Zambia's oldest stone church building.

PLACES TO STAY

The Haven, Tel: (04) 455103
Email: ckachese@zamnet.zm
Newcomer, just off main street in Mpulungu, camping among tropical plants, self-catering chalets. Boat trips, snorkelling, fishing, scuba diving.

Kasakalawe Lodge, Tel: (04) 221615
Email: steth@zamnet.zm
Located on the lake.

Mishembe, Tel: (04) 221615
Email: steth@zamnet.zm
A small private secluded beach at the base of Kalambo Falls. Access is by boat. Only tented accommodation is available with either. catering or self catering.

Mbita Rest House, Tel: (04) 455057, Fax: (04) 455135. Hostel accommodation.

Nkupi Lodge, Tel: (04) 455166
Situated on the edge of the town, popular spot for backpackers & campers. Self catering.

Tanganyika Lodge

Situated on a beautiful stretch of rocky lakeshore. It has three twin chalets, two ensuite family chalets & camping facilities.

LAKE TANGANIKA

Local legend has it that the lake was once a bottomless well, stocked with a variety of fish. It was owned by a man and his wife who had been told that if they revealed the existence of the well to anyone, a disaster would befall them. But the woman, who had a lover, revealed the secret to him. When she did so the waters of the well rose so high that they drowned everyone and formed Lake Tanganyika.

Perhaps as old as 15 million years, Lake Tanganyika is a place of breathtaking natural beauty - of cloudless skies, crystal clear blue waters, deserted golden beaches and fiery sunsets. But its waters are also temperamental and the weather changes frequently stirring up some awesome and dangerous storms.

At its deepest, the lake goes down to 1470m, making it the second deepest lake in the world after Lake Baikal in Siberia. At 675km, it's the longest fresh water lake on earth. The surface layers of the lake are tropical and support all sorts of life, including the many species of colourful cichlid fish, the sort that you see in aquariums all over the world. Deeper waters don't get the sunlight . Over the years the lake has been the scene of bloody wars, a flourishing Arab slave trade and even a naval battle between the British and Germans during the First World War.

It's a wonderful place to snorkel or even scuba dive, because of the beautiful multi-coloured fish, but beware of the hippos and crocodiles. It's also a prime fishing spot, the furthest south for the goliath tigerfish or Nile perch, which can reach 80kg, is full of nkupi, the largest cichlids in the world, and, due to its isolation, boasts 500 species, many of which are endemic. Best fishing is between March and November, and unsurprisingly the lake is the venue for the annual Zambia National Fishing Competition, usually held in April.

The best place to stay is **Kasaba Bay Lodge** which is top of the range.
Telefax: (27) 11 7877700,
Email: inbound@iafrica.com
A lodge geared up for fishing, keen anglers come from all over Zambia. Chalets line the lake. Boats and fishing tackle can be hired and it has its own airstrip.

NSUMBU NATIONAL PARK

On the southern shore of the lake is the beautiful but remote Nsumbu park, a mix of hilly grasslands, escarpement and wetlands.

From Mpulungu you can get to the park by boat.

The journey takes about 12 hours in small unreliable boats. From elsewhere, you need to fly.

Chartered planes land at Kasaba Bay airstrip. For the more hardy travellers, drive 160km from Kasama to Mporokoso over a very difficult road, from where it is 180km to Nsumbu. The journey will take all day.

The park is really a fishing rather than an animal paradise - poachers wiped out most of the game – and fishing enthusiasts rate it as one of the best places for freshwater fishing on the continent.

Located in a spectacular position on wooded hillside overlooking the lake, just north of the Nsumbu Park is **Ndole Bay Lodge** Tel: (02) 711150/096 780196, Fax: (02) 711390 *Email: ndolebay@coppernet.zm;* Ensuite chalets, plus campsite under trees on the beach, boat launching facilites and a swimming pool.

KABWELUMA FALLS

CHIPEMPE RAPIDS.

104 YR OLD NGONI WOMAN

COPPERBELT & NORTH WEST

Zambia was built on the back of copper and the Copperbelt is where all the action was, and, hopefully, will be again.

It is the main centre of population outside the capital Lusaka and one of the most urbanised places in Africa, but sadly, the fortunes of Zambia's industrial heart have declined with the demise of the copper mines. Copperbelt towns are no longer the vibrant and dynamic centers that they were. There are new investors in the mines with exploration activties wide spread. There are a few attractions for visitors most notably Chimfunshi Chimpanzee Sanctuary and the open pit mine in Chingola.

The main cities of the Copperbelt are Ndola and Kitwe and smaller towns include Luanshya, Chililabombwe, Mufulira and Chingola.

KABWE

Travelling by road, the 320km journey to Ndola on the Great North Road, you pass through the small town of Kabwe. This is where Zambia's most famous prehistoric Broken Hill Man was found in the 1920s. Places to stay are:-

Tuskers Hotel
Tel: (05) 222076 -7/ 222498,
Fax: (05) 222076
Email: tuskers@zamnet.zm
Situated in the centre of town. Simple and quality ensuite accommodation, restaurant, lounge bar, swimming pool. Conference facilities available.

Kabwe Lodge Tel: (05) 224297, Fax: (05) 224297, Located on Marshal Street, on the outskirts of town. Offers basic conference facilities with swimming pool.

Zambezi Source Lodge Tel: (05) 223286/ 222597, Fax: (05) 224020, 1590 Natuseko Rd

CPCU Motel Fax: (05) 222153/224020

Masiye Motel Tel: (05) 223221/221500, Fax: (05) 223221
Simple and provides the basic facilities required.

KAPIRI MPOSHI

About 200km north of Kabwe to the Copperbelt, is Kapiri Mposhi, a small but busy town where you can stock up on basics here.

For train passengers to Tanzania on the Tazara, Kapiri is the starting point, at the station, just north of the town centre is **Kapiri Motel**, Tel: (05) 271356/48

Lake Kashiba

Continuing north of Kapiri Mposhi about 32km on the way to Ndola is **Lake Kashiba**. A local beauty spot, Lake Kashiba offers basic camping facilities. It is a natural sunken lake, about 800m across and over 100m deep, revered by the local people. It is also possible to swim in the lake, which has no crocodiles. You can also go bird watching in the nearby forest.

About an hours' drive from Ndola on the road to Lusaka is **Nsobe Game Ranch**, well-signposted. Lovely game park where you can go for a drive, have lunch and stay overnight. Tel: (02) 610113

OPEN PIT MINE

NDOLA

Ndola is Zambia's third largest city, after Kitwe and Lusaka, and the administrative capital of the Copperbelt region, although it was never a major mining town but rather a base for manufacturing.

The international airport is a sign of the historic importance of Ndola Nowadays, its factories are closed and there is not much to attract the visitor.

If you are in town, check out the Slave Tree in Makoli Avenue, a backstreet near the railway line. The tree stands as a reminder of the cruel trade in human beings. This mupapa (Afzelia quanzesis) was not only a shaded meeting point for Swahili traders, but also a place for them to buy and sell slaves. The Slave Tree features on the coat of arms of the city of Ndola.

The small Copperbelt Museum on Buteko Avenue has exhibits from the ancient and modern copper industries, such as smelting equipment, and a now somewhat bedraggled but nevertheless impressive butterfly collection. There are also cultural artefacts and a small selection of curios for sale.

HOW TO GET THERE

By Air

There are daily flights to Ndola from Lusaka (US$105 one way) and daily flights from Johannesburg. Also twice weekly from Mansa/Kasama.
Ndola Interational Airport
Tel: (02) 611193 / 611194,
Fax: (02) 612635

By Road

There are several luxury coaches a day from Lusaka to Ndola. The Post Bus goes daily to Kasama in Northern Province - inquire at the post office. See General Tips on pages 78 - 84 for the different Travel and Tour operators which are situated in this region.

THINGS TO DO

A vist to the Copperbelt Museum on Buteko Avenue is worthwhile. Tel: (02) 613591 /617727, Fax: (02) 617450/617727

Just outside of town, on the Misundu road is the Brown's farm, where the owners have set up Gecko Gallery. A gallery and shop with a good selection of reasonably priced locally-made jewellery arts and crafts. There's also a coffee shop with delicious cakes. Tel: (02) 622241

About 10 kilometres from Ndola on the road to Kitwe is the Dag Hammerskjold Memorial.

This memorial site marks the site of the tragic plane crash, in which the Swedish Secretary General of the United Nations, Dag Hammerskjold, died on 18 September, 1961 while on a peace mediation mission to the troubled Katanga region of the present day Democratic Republic of Congo. Be careful as armed bandits have been known to operate in the area. Also on the Kitwe road, standing right in the middle of the dual carriageway, is the Chichele Mofu Tree. Reputed to be over 200 years old, local legend has it that this tree houses the spirit of a long-dead chief.

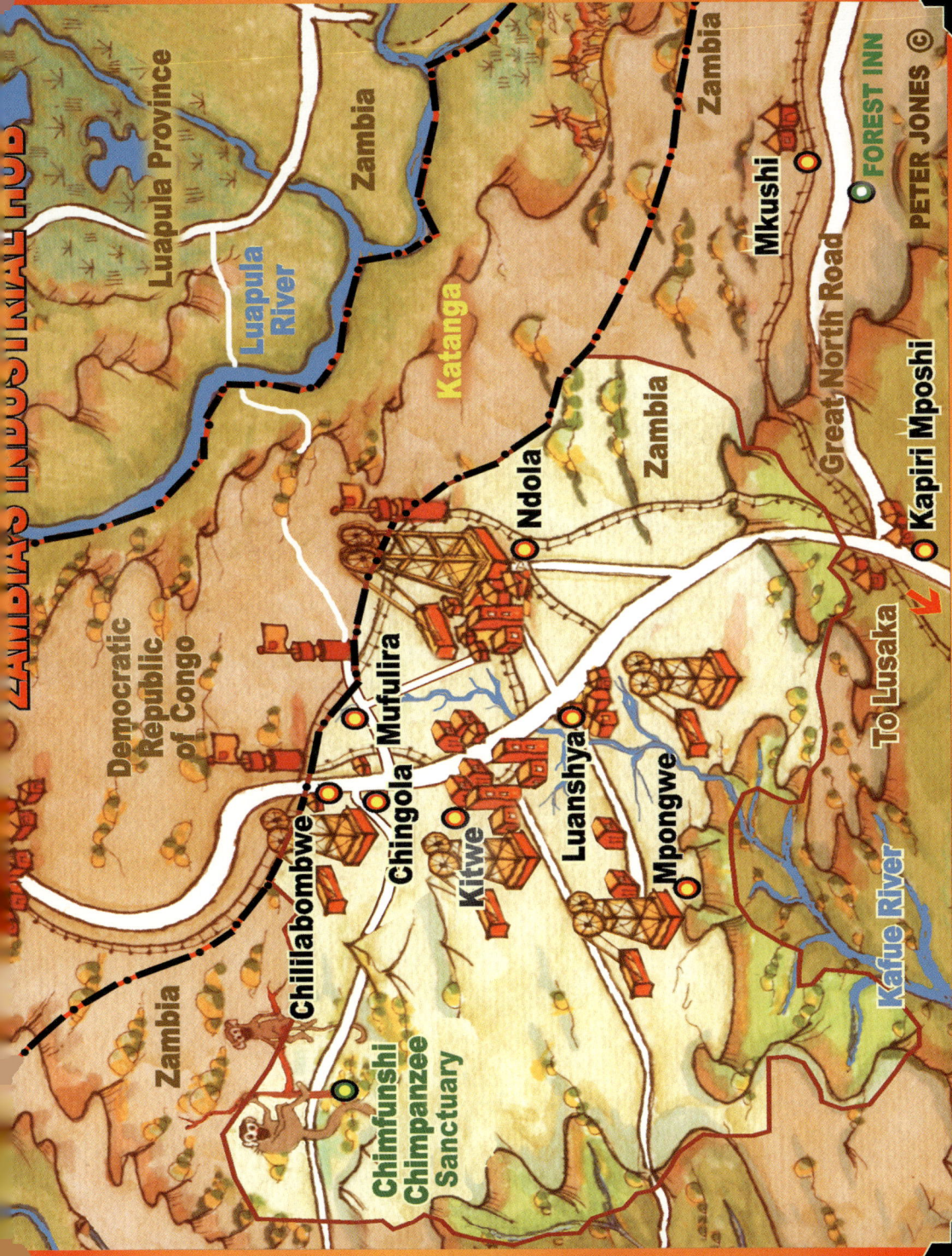

ZAMBIA'S INDUSTRIAL HUB

Luapula Province

Zambia

Luapula River

Zambia

Katanga

Zambia

Ndola

Democratic Republic of Congo

Mufulira

Chingola

Chililabombwe

Kitwe

Luanshya

Mpongwe

Zambia

Chimfunshi Chimpanzee Sanctuary

Mkushi

Great North Road

Kapiri Mposhi

To Lusaka

Kafue River

Middle Range

Michelangelo
Hotel, Café & Restaurant

Michelangelo Hotel, Tel: (02) 620325 /620476, Fax: (02) 620326
Email: vgstyle@zamnet.zm
126 Broadway Avenue
Ensuite bedrooms with air conditioning, and mini bar service. Adjacent to the Michelangelo Italian restaurant. Swimming pool.

Mukuba Hotel, Tel: (02) 651000/2/3, Fax: (02) 651006/651012
Email: mukhotel@zamtel.zm
Located within the Ndola Trade Fair grounds, adorned with impala. All rooms are ensuite with air conditioning, swimmimg pool, bar, restaurant and gym.

Budget

The Palm Guest House
Tel: (02) 680725 /680187
Fax: (02) 680187
Email: palmguest@zamtel.zm
4753 Mukuni Rd, Kansenshi
Ensuite bedrooms. Situated only 10 minutes away from the Ndola International Airport & a stone's throw from the city centre.

Royal Hotel

Royal Hotel, Tel: (02) 621840/3, Fax: (02) 621850
Email: royhotel@zamtel.zm
Plot B10 Vitanda Street
Previously the CopperSmith Arms, family atmosphere with ensuite air conditioned rooms and satellite TV.

Good Night Guest House
Tel: (02) 660313, Fax: (02) 660313
Located in main town and provides the basic facilities.

Henry Makulu House
Tel: (02) 610149 /612261
Fax: (02) 610149, Yembe Rd,
Former government hostel.

Ndola Executive Lodge
Tel: (02) 640378, Fax: (02) 640378
Email: maya@zamnet.zm
33 Sheila Dare Road, Northrise.
7 pleasant self contained rooms in converted house.

New Ambassador Hotel
Tel: (02) 617071/ 617134,
Fax: (02) 617134
E- Mail: ambasshotel@zamtel.zm
Located within town on President's Avenue has basic ensuite twin, double and family rooms.

The Savoy Hotel
Tel: (02) 611097/8, Fax: (02) 614001
Email: savoy@zamnet.zm
Located in the centre of town on Buteko Avenue, all rooms are ensuite.

Setanga Lodge
Tel: (02) 680002/ 096 780325,
Fax: (02) 680002,
Email: setanga@zamnet.zm
578H Freedom Way, Kansenshi
Comfortable rooms with satellite TV. Swimming pool and secure parking.

ZESCO Guest House Tel: (02) 611705/ 613160, Fax: (02) 611709

WHERE TO EAT

Michelangelo
Hotel, Café & Restaurant

Michelangelo Tel: (02) 620325/6,
Fax: (02) 620325
Plot 126 Broadway Road
Email: vgstyle@zamnet.zm
Good Italian restaurant/café serving pizzas and other traditional Italian fare.

Danny's Restaurant
Tel: (02) 621828/ 610347
President Avenue
Good value Indian food, pleasant atmosphere. Best bet for a meal out.

Hong Kong Restaurant
Tel: (02) 614014,
President Avenue
One of the oldest Chinese restaurant in Ndola.

LUANSHYA

One of the oldest colonial mine towns in the country that thrived during the peak mining era.

Located just off the road between Ndola and Kitwe, on the northern edge of Luanshya, is **Lowden Lodge**, a former colonial farmhouse which offers pleasant accommodation in garden cottages. Tel: (02) 515001/ 096 781105/ 096 781105, Fax: (02) 515054 *Email: lowden@coppernet.zm*; Located on the Kitwe road after the Fisenge turnoff, 20km from Ndola is the **Baluba Motel** Tel: (096) 784632/ 02 515009, Fax: (02) 612080
Email:muyanco@zamnet.zm

KITWE

Some 60km from Ndola on the dual carriageway is Kitwe, Zambia's second city. It is a well laid-out city with hotels, restaurants, nightclubs and good sporting facilities. The city owes its existence to the discovery of copper in the 1920s and grew in wealth and importance with the development of copper production in the area.

Even today its fortunes are still heavily tied to the copper industry. You can arrange a trip down the mines. Other than the mines, there is little for visitors, but if you enjoy peace and beauty about 20km on the road to Kalulushi is the *Chembe Bird Sanctuary*. Run by the Wildlife and Environment Conservation Society of Zambia, Chembe Bird Sanctuary is a wooded sanctuary with a beautiful lake, camping and boating facilities.

You can also fish, although if catch smaller fish they must be returned to the water quickly, and you can also have a picnic or braai. Tel: (02) 228914 / (096) 908119.

Some birds to be seen, are the white pelican, Squacco heron, Hammerkop,

African pygmy goose, European hobby, Meyers parrot & many more. This place is ideal for picnics, bar-be-ques and weekend camping.

By air

The South Downs airport is presently under renovations, there are three daily flights from Lusaka to Ndola, road transfer to Kitwe.

By road

There are several luxury coaches everyday to Kitwe from Lusaka via Ndola.

Middle Range

The Town House Lodge
Tel: (02) 221855,
Fax: (02) 221855
Email: superior@zamtel.zm
65A Mabvuto Close, Parklands
Executive suite, double ensuite rooms, single rooms with shared bathroom. Mini bar in all rooms.

Africaza Guest House
Tel: (02) 221097, Fax: (02) 226842
11 Mushitu Close, off Nationlist Way
Beautifully set with facilities for the executive traveller. Restaurant on site.

Copperbelt Energy Corporation Guest House Tel: (02) 244185/244301,
Fax: (02) 244353
Email: guesthouse@cec.co.zm
1 Broadway Avenue, CEC Village
Furnished self-contained rooms.

Copperfields Guest House
Tel: (02) 230710 /230709,
Fax: (02) 231027
Email: copperfields@zamnet.zm
48 Freedom Avenue, Parklands
Double-storey building, self-contained rooms with the Copperpot restaurant.

Hotel Edinburgh, Tel: (02) 222444,
Fax: (02) 225036, Obote Avenue
Email: edin@coppernet.zm
Website: www.hoteledin.co.za
Has rooms to suit all ranges. Conference facilities available and swimming pool.

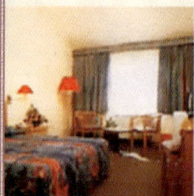

Rosewood Place, Tel: (02) 220027-8,
Fax: (02) 220029
Email: rosewoodplace@zamnet.zm
Plot 1478, Luangwa Walk, Parklands
Self-catering apartments, single and doubles, furnished, with equipped kitchens.
DSTV, telephone and English breakfast.

La Paillotte Guest House
Tel: (02) 220650, Fax: (02) 220650
30 Kanyanta Avenue
Nice and clean with all the basic amenities available. Pleasant surroundings.

Sherbourne Guest House
Tel: (02) 230548/222168,
Fax: (02) 226477
Email: sherbo@zamnet.zm
20 Pamo Avenue, Parklands
Just north of the city centre, an established guesthouse with conference facilities, bar and pleasant garden restaurant.

Budget

Blue Gates Guest House
Tel: 095 908620 / 884666 / 097 758217,
Email:bguest@zamtel.zm
amushinga@yahoo.com
3 Chikuni Crescent, Parklands
Located in the heart of Kitwe.

BLUE GATES
GUEST HOUSE
OUR HOME AWAY FROM HOME

Eagle Guest House
Tel:(02)229748/230761 /230777, Fax: (02) 230153
Email: gayatech@zamnet.zm
Website: www.gayatech.co.zm
22 Fraser Crescent, Riverside
Single and double self-contained rooms.

Eagle Guest House
Your Home on the Copperbelt

The Diamond Lodge
Tel: (02) 220294,
Fax: (02) 220294
Email: dlodge@zamnet.zm
14 Diamond Crescent, Martindale Area

House of Jas-min
Tel:(02) 215124/ 210134,
Fax: (02) 211142
Email: jasmin@coppernet.zm
4650 Jasmine Close, Buyantanshi
All rooms are self contained.

Lothian House
Tel: (02) 222889,
Fax: (02) 222889
Plot 22, Chandamali Avenue, Parklands

Gil Guest House
Tel: (02) 230309/096 780592,
Fax: (02) 230809
5056 Zebra Close, Nkana East

Greenlane Guest House
Tel: (02) 222769 / 223651,
Fax: (02) 225882 , 2 Pamo Avenue
Email: w.m.mumba@zamnet.zm

Jubilee Lodge and Restaurant
Tel: (02) 230610,
Fax: (02) 230610/227033
Email: jubilee@zamnet.zm
Located within the Kitwe Show Grounds.

Mukwa Guest House
Tel: (02) 224266 /230393,
Fax: (02) 230389,
Email: mukwa@coppernet.zm,
26/28 Mpezeni Avenue, Parklands
Self-contained rooms and swimming pool.

KITWE

NORTH

ITIMPI

RACE COURSE

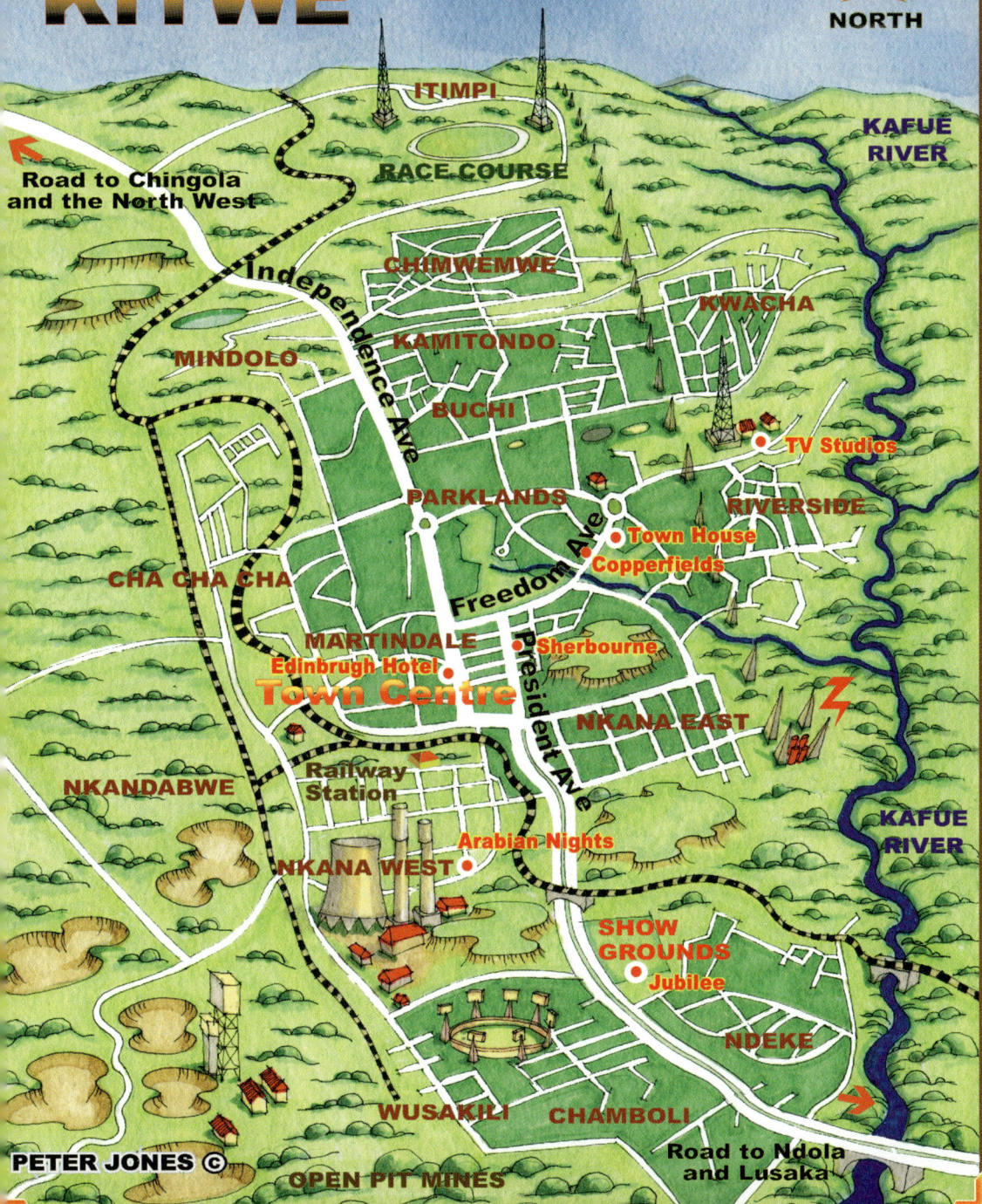

← Road to Chingola
and the North West

CHIMWEMWE

KWACHA

KAMITONDO

MINDOLO

BUCHI

TV Studios

PARKLANDS

RIVERSIDE

Town House

Copperfields

CHA CHA CHA

Freedom Ave

MARTINDALE

Sherbourne

Edinbrugh Hotel

Town Centre

NKANA EAST

Railway
Station

Arabian Nights

NKANDABWE

KAFUE
RIVER

NKANA WEST

SHOW
GROUNDS

Jubilee

NDEKE

WUSAKILI

CHAMBOLI

PETER JONES ©

OPEN PIT MINES

Road to Ndola
and Lusaka

KAFUE
RIVER

Independence Ave

President Ave

ZCCM Guest House Tel: (02) 215495, Fax: (02) 245437/218108

YMCA Norfred House Hostels
Tel: (02) 215495 / 095 914672,
Fax: (02) 218108
1231 Kew Gardens, Parklands
Email: ymcahost@zamnet.zm

WHERE TO EAT

Acropolis Taverna ,Tel: (02) 220664 /220703, Fax: (02) 229329,
Wenye Road
Good Mediterranean cuisine.

Africaza Restaurant
Tel: (02) 221097, Fax: (02) 226842
11 Mushitu Close, off Nationlist Way,
Parklands

Jubilee Restaurant
Tel: (02) 230610, Fax: (02) 230610 /227033, Kitwe – Ndola Rd

La Paillotte Restaurant
Tel: (02) 220650, Fax: (02) 220650
30 Kanyanta Avenue

CHINGOLA

From Kitwe, it is a distance of 52km to the mining town of *Chingola*. There are several luxury coaches a day from Kitwe to Lusaka via Ndola or from Lusaka to Kitwe. From Kitwe you can take a bus or taxi to Chingola. Chingola is known for its fine golf course, which was once ranked amongst the finest golf courses in Southern Africa.

It also has hotels, motels, guesthouses and shops. There are some new developments in the town including a new modern Protea hotel and improved banking facilities. But this mini-boom has slowed down since the withdrawal in 2002 of the mining company Anglo American.

Chingola is mainly used as a stop-over

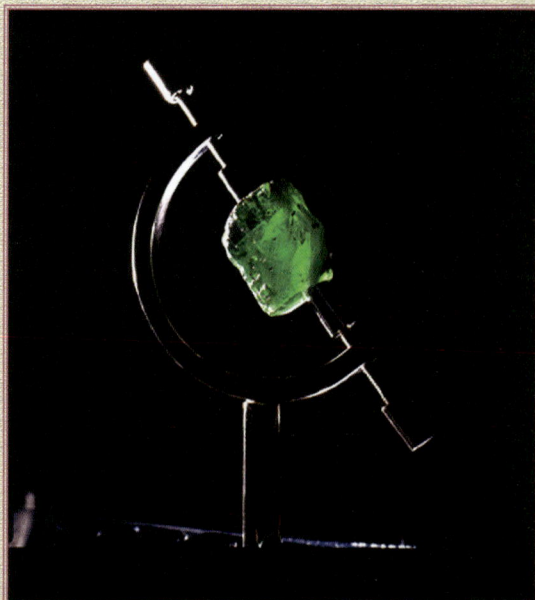

point for those visiting the wonderful Chimfunshi Chimpanzee Sanctuary.

Middle Range

Protea Hotel,
Tel:(02)312810/310624-5,
Fax: (02) 313510,
Kabundi Rd
Email: protea@za,tel.zm
Website: www.proteahotels.com
Ideal for the business visitor. Conference facilities available

Rosewood Guest House,
Tel: (02) 313114 / (096) 786131/096 909985, Fax: (02) 313114,
47 President Avenue
Email: rosewood@zamnet.zm
Pleasant secure premises. Self-contained rooms with satellite TV and swimming pool.

Budget

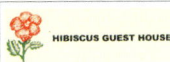

Hibiscus Guest House
Tel: (02) 313635 /(096) 781045,
Fax: (02) 313635, 33/35 Katutwa Street.
Situated in a secure residential area. Satellite TV, swimming pool.

Lima Motel Tel: (02) 313380,
Fax: (02) 311660, Plot 1902, Kitwe Road
Email: limamotel@zamtel.zm

The Willows Tel: (096) 786140,
Fax: (02) 312432, 57 President Avenue

CHIMFUNSHI CHIMPANZEE SANCTUARY

From Chingola take the road towards Solwezi for about 50km till you get to the signpost for Chimfunshi, turn right and continue along the gravel, which is sometimes in a bad state, for a short distance. Beside the Kafue river, award-winning Chimfunshi is the largest chimpanzee sanctuary in the world. This impressive chimpanzee sanctuary run by a remarkable couple, Dave and Sheila Siddle, is well worth the trek, to see for yourself just how similar humans are to chimps. Chimpanzees are not indigenous to Zambia and most of Chimfunshi's residents have been rescued: some were smuggled out of the jungle of Democratic Republic of Congo destined to America or Europe, others from zoos around the world. There are over 70 chimps in the sanctuary, 17 of which were born there. The sanctuary expanded in April 2000, with the addition of two 200-hectare enclosures of natural forest and grassland for groups of up to 30 chimps to wander around in. The new enclosures are about 6km away from the main enclosure. Chimfunshi has an educational centre that focuses on teaching school children about the chimpanzees and their environment. Don't just turn up; Chimfunshi is not geared up for a large number of tourists. Phone ahead (02) 311293 , or arrange a visit through a travel agency. There's a simple camp-site and the education centre has dorm beds and self-catering facilities. And don't visit if you're ill, chimps can catch human diseases and in 1999 two chimps died from the flu virus, probably picked up from a visitor. For more information, email *chimps@yebo.co.za* and visit the *website www.chimfunshi.org.za*

Solwezi is a logical stop for the more hardy traveller determined to see the source of the Zambezi River. Solwezi is a large lively town with a large market, shops and restaurants but with no pull for tourists beyond being a stepping stone to the source of the Zambezi, the remote outpost of Mwininlunga or the privately-run Nchila Wildlife Reserve (*www.nchila-wildlife-reserve.com*). You will need to book well in advance if you want to visit Nchila.

Changa Changa Motel Tel: (08) 821300/ 297, Fax: (08) 821300; **Sakatenga and Sons Motel**, Tel: (08) 821745; **Twafikako Guest House**, Tel: (08) 821275

Some 400 or so km south-west of Solwezi is the small and basic town of Kabompo. Its claim to fame is its honey, harvested from surrounding forests and of such good quality that it is exported as far afield as Europe. On the banks of the Zambezi River and close to Angola, the town of Zambezi is about 71 km from Kabompo. There are simple guest hous-es, some shops, government offices and a bank. Approximately 2 km east of Zambezi is the Luvale royal capital of Mize.

CHINYINGI BRIDGE

About 30 km from Zambezi heading toward Chavuma is a track leading to the Capuchin mission at Chinyingi.

The mission shares its name with the well known landmark and remarkable engineering feat of Chinyingi Bridge, at 700ft one of the longest suspension bridges over the river Zambezi. It is hard to believe that this bridge was built almost 50 years ago by Brother Crispin from the mission and a team of local workers who had no formal technical training. It was built after a number of people, including some from the mis-sion, drowned while they were crossing the river by boat at night. The bridge is built from cables and pipes which were sourced from the mines on the Copperbelt over 600km away. Joining the pedestrians across the bridge, espe-cially at sunset, is a memorable experi-ence . Head northwest of Solwezi if you want to reach the source of the Zambezi River. After about 35km from Solwezi, the road splits at Mutanda, take the right fork heading west for 240km until you reach the town of Mwinilunga. At the heart of a pineapple-growing region, Mwininlunga is a small place, with sim-ple guesthouses, a bank, fuel station and a few shops.

Beaumont Lodge, Tel: (08) 361006; **Zambezi Motel**, Tel: (08) 321511, Fax: (08) 371026. Some 50km west of Mwinilunga is the source of the Zambezi, the starting point of this great river's 2,700km journey to the Indian Ocean. The place is a truly historic site.

DIPLOMATIC MISSIONS

Angolan Embassy, Tel (01) 234761,
Fax (01) 234763,
Serval road, Kabulonga

Botswana High Commission,
Tel (01) 250555/ 250019,
Fax (01) 253895,Pandit Nehru road,
Email:- wamep@mailcity.com

Egyptian Embassy, Tel (01) 250229,
Fax (01) 254149, Plot 5206
United Nations Ave.

Kenya High Commission, Tel (01)
250722/250742, Fax (01) 253829,
United Nations Ave, Plot 5207.
Email:- kenhigh@zamnet.zm

Mozambique High Commission,
Tel (01) 239135, Fax (01) 220345,
9592 Kwacha road, North mead,
Email: mozhlsk@zamnet.zm

Namibian High Commission,
Tel (01) 260407/8, Fax (01) 263858,
Plot 30B, Mutende road, Woodlands.
Email:namibia@coppernet.zm

Nigerian High Commission,
Tel (01) 253177/253265, Fax (01)
253915, Hailie Selassie Ave.

South African High Commission,
Tel (01) 260999, Fax (01) 263001,
26D Cheeta road Kabulonga,
Email: sacb@zamnet.zm

Zimbabwe High Commission,
Tel (01) 254012 /254006,
Fax (01) 254046, Haile Selassie Ave.
Email:- zimzam@coppernet.zm

U.S.A. Embassy,
Tel (01) 252305, Fax (01) 252225,
Corner of Independence & United
Nations Ave.
Email: embpas@zamnet.zm

Canadian High Commission,
Tel (01) 250833, Fax (01) 254176,5199
United Nations Ave, Longacres
Email: lsaka@dfait-maeci.gc.ca

Cuban Embassy,
Tel (01) 291308, Fax (01) 291586, 5574
Magoye road,Kalundu
Email: mache@zamnet.zm

Chinese Embassy,
Tel (01) 253770 /251169,
Fax (01) 251157,
United Nations Ave, Longacres

Indian Embassy,
Tel (01) 253066 /253152-9,
Fax (01) 254118,1 Pandit Nehru Rd,
Longacres.

Japanese Embassy,
Tel (01) 251555 /254451,
Fax (01) 253488,
Haile Selassie Ave,
Email: jez@zamtel.zm

244

NGONI WARRIORS

EUROPEAN UNION COUNTRIES

British High Commission,
Tel (01) 251133/251923,
Fax (01) 253798, Independence Ave,
Email: british@zamnet.zm

Royal Danish Embassy,
Tel (01) 254277, Fax (01) 254618,
Manenekela road,
off Independence Avenue
Email:- lunamb@um.dk

Netherlands Embassy, Tel (01)
253994/253818, Fax (01) 253733,
United Nations Ave,
Email: nlgovlus@zamnet.zm

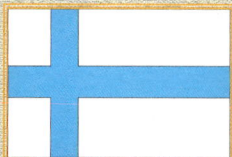

Finish Embassy, Tel (01) 251234/
251988, Fax (01) 253783,
Haile Selassie Ave, Opp Ndeke Hse,
Email: finemb@zamnet.zm

French Embassy,
Tel (01) 251322 /253808,
Fax (01) 254475, 4th Floor Anglo
American Building, Plot 74
Independence Ave,
Email:- france@ambfrance-zm.org

German Embassy,
Tel (01) 251259 /250644,
Fax (01) 254014, United Nations Ave,
Plot 5209, *Email: germany@zamtel.zm*

Irish Embassy,
Tel (01) 290650 /291124,
Fax (01) 290482,
6663 Katima Mulilo road.
Olympia Extention
Email:- iremb@zamnet.zm

Italian Embassy,
Tel (01) 250781/ 250755
Fax (01) 254929,
Diplomatic Traingle
next to British High Commission
Email: italyzam@zamnet.zm

ANTIQUE CRATFS

Swedish Embassy,
Tel (01) 251249 /251711,
Fax (01) 254049,
Haile Selassie Ave, Opp Ndeke Hse.
Email: ambassaden.lusaka@sidd.se

Switzerland Consulate,
Tel (01) 223838,
Fax (01) 223845,
Off Great North road,
behind Impala service station
Email: imstr@eml-eis.com

OTHER EUROPEAN COUNTRIES

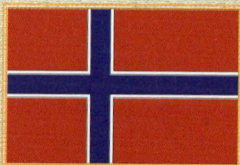

Royal Norwegian Embassy,
Tel (01) 252625-6/252188, Fax (01)
253915, Dunduza Chisidza road.
Email: lunamb@um.bk

Cyprit Consulate,
Tel (01) 262931
Roan road,
Kabulonga

248

Great East road and Manchinchi road
Telephone: 01 255550, Fax: 01 255551
Email: mandahill @zamnet.zm
mandahill@zamtel.zm

TO ORDER
"THE MAGIC OF ZAMBIA"
Travellers Guide

CONTACT:

IMAGE PROMOTIONS
Tel +260 1 223344
fax +260 1 236585
Email: image@zamtel.zm
www.magic-of-zambia.com

P. O. Box 36383
Lusaka
Zambia